Fiducial Governance

An Australian republic for the new millennium

Fiducial Governance

An Australian republic for the new millennium

John Power

THE AUSTRALIAN NATIONAL UNIVERSITY

E PRESS

Published by ANU E Press
The Australian National University
Canberra ACT 0200, Australia
Email: anuepress@anu.edu.au
This title is also available online at: http://epress.anu.edu.au/fiducial_citation.html

National Library of Australia
Cataloguing-in-Publication entry

Author:	Power, John (John Marcus)
Title:	Fiducial governance : an Australian republic for the new millennium / John Power.
ISBN:	9781921666544 (pbk.) 9781921666551 (eBook)
Series:	ANZSOG series.
Notes:	Includes bibliographical references and index.
Subjects:	Republicanism--Australia. Democracy--Australia. Australia--Politics and government.
Dewey Number:	321.860994

Cover design by John Butcher

Funding for this monograph series has been provided by the Australia and New Zealand School of Government Research Program.

John Wanna, *Series Editor*

Professor John Wanna is the Sir John Bunting Chair of Public Administration at the Research School of Social Sciences at The Australian National University and is the director of research for the Australian and New Zealand School of Government (ANZSOG). He is also a joint appointment with the Department of Politics and Public Policy at Griffith University and a principal researcher with two research centres: the Governance and Public Policy Research Centre and the nationally-funded Key Centre in Ethics, Law, Justice and Governance at Griffith University.

Contents

Foreword

For those of us with a commitment to a republican Australia, this monograph presents a fresh approach. In developing its framework for constitutional reform, it draws on a range of ideas – not only republican, but Indigenous, feminist, and religious thinking as well.

As an Indigenous Australian I am very committed to reform within Australian political institutions. In my former role as Aboriginal and Torres Strait Islander Social Justice Commissioner I facilitated a reform agenda that ultimately led to the formation of the National Congress of Australia's First Peoples. The abolition of the Aboriginal and Torres Strait Islander Commission (ATSIC) in 2004 left Indigenous Australians without an institutional mechanism to represent our interests at a national and international levels. This event also gave cause to some considerable soul searching within the Indigenous polity. It was clear that Indigenous Australians wanted an institutional mechanism that would represent our interests. There was also much debate about how this might be developed and much to be learnt from the apparent flaws both in earlier attempts to achieve this vision – including the ATSIC model and a contemporary, government selected and appointed, Indigenous advisory body.

Our approach to the development of the three-chamber model for the National Congress for Australia's First Peoples was in the first instance framed by Article 18 of the United Nations Declaration which mandates that Indigenous peoples should have a determining role in the development of political structures to represent their interests. There were a number of principles that informed the design of the National Congress. There were, for example, the problems that can arise with low participation in voluntary elections and the need to ensure a capable representative structure with Indigenous accountabilities. Such accountabilities include gender equality, open and transparent two-way communications between the people and the Congress, adoption of an ethics monitoring mechanism and adoption of guiding principles. In developing this model we aimed to take advantage of existing Indigenous structures without comprising their political integrity. I believe that it is a unique model and I am very pleased that it has in some way influenced Power's thinking on the challenging but important issues explored in this book.

Of course, few people will agree with everything Power has to say. I, for one, remain more optimistic than he is about the prospects of attaining a republic in our lifetimes. Nevertheless, he alerts us to the need for the great deal of hard work and further dialogue before we can gain a genuinely republican nation.

In the process of doing this hard work, we should be able to advance on other fronts as well. For example, I can now see new ways in which the cause of reconciliation could be furthered as we progress to the republic: for example, if only our governments followed Power's advice on fiducial governance and adopted explicit policies and practices aimed at enhancing public trust in them! Should they commit to doing this, it would be far from fanciful to hope that our first Australian President will be an Indigenous Australian!

Dr Tom Calma
DLett (h.c.) CD

About the author

John Power holds the degrees of BA (Hons) University of Melbourne; and AM and PhD (Harvard University). He has held a variety of academic positions at the Universities of Melbourne and Sydney, the Canberra College of Advanced Education, the Australian National University, RMIT, Canberra and Victoria Universities. He has also held leadership positions in the Institute of Public Administration, the Research Committee of the Structure and Organization of Government Research Committee of the International Political Science Association, and the Victorian Local Governance Association. His most recent major publication was the 2007 volume co-authored with John Halligan and Robin Miller and published by Melbourne University Press – *Parliament in the Twenty-first Century* – which won the 2007 Richard Baker prize for the work that best promoted 'understanding of the Senate and its work'.

Acknowledgments

I have written this monograph for my grandchildren, in the hope that it might assist them and their generation in the securing of a worthwhile republic in Australia before the end of this century.

For helpful comments during the long period of gestation of this monograph, I wish to thank Ian Anderson, Peter Boyce, John Burke, Glyn Davis, Tom Davis, Grant Duncan, Geoff Gallop, Bob Gregory, John Halligan, Toby Halligan, Harshan Kumarasingham, David Latimer, the late Richard McGarvie, John Nethercote, Marcus Power, Jenny Stewart, John Wanna, John Warhurst and Roger Wettenhall.

My greatest debt is to Ann Morrow, who scrutinised the entire draft and made many helpful suggestions.

Finally, my thanks are due to the University of Melbourne, which provided a well-equipped office and access to library services throughout the work on this project. I would also like to record my appreciation of the professional way in which my manuscript has been edited for publication by Jan Borrie and John Butcher's assistance and advice in relation to the publication process.

Anyone scanning the list of aforementioned colleagues will soon realise that there are many points at which most of them would disagree with my argument. They have all, however, provided me with useful feedback. All deficiencies of the work remain my responsibility.

Preface

Reinventing parliamentary democracy for a differentiated polity in the twenty-first century is a task scarcely begun, in either theory or practice...It is perhaps more a wonder, given the shackles they wear, that leaders achieve anything at all. (Rhodes 1997:222)

When an earlier draft of some of this monograph was circulated to two readers—both of whom I respect for their different mixes of academic and practical skills—the feedback I received was encouraging but concerning. Both readers considered that my argument was a weighty one but so 'out of left field' that it would be difficult to attract a wide audience of concerned citizens to consider my proposals. So the purpose of this brief preface is to present some of the key points in what follows in this monograph, in the hope that it might encourage perseverance among readers who might otherwise be put off by my introduction and theoretical framework-setting Section 1. Alternatively, those readers who are interested mainly in the ways in which Australia could best proceed to a republican regime might prefer to go straight to Section 2.

a) The Geertzian challenge

I am here attempting to respond to a challenge issued some years ago by the eminent anthropologist Clifford Geertz. A few years before his death, Geertz threw down the gauntlet to political theorists wishing to embark on the design of governance regimes suited to the new millennium. In his stimulating essay 'The world in pieces: culture and politics at the end of the century', Geertz (2000:235) emphasised the 'disassembly of the bipolar world' with an increasingly messy and uneven multiculturalism cutting across national boundaries. In his view, a new form of politics was needed (Geertz 2000:245), and a new form of political theorising to accompany it. This new form of theorising should eschew over-hasty generalisation and should flow from concerns with existing institutions and practices and their inadequacies. He convincingly contended that all the major writers in the grand tradition of political theorising—from Plato to Rousseau—had been creatively stimulated by the pressing nature of the problems faced by the regimes in which they lived (Geertz 2000:219).

One of Rousseau's contemporaries—the governance practitioner and theorist Montesquieu—has proven to be the most heavily influential thinker on modern constitution making, so much so that some of his most important propositions have become deeply embedded in the contemporary republican assumptive world. It is therefore appropriate for me to begin my response to the Geertzian challenge with a brief critique of a key Montesquieu proposition. In this way, I shall attempt to illustrate what I consider should be one of the most important features of republican thinking—the constant questioning of key assumptions—while at the same time setting an important part of the context for the argument that follows.

b) Questioning Montesquieu

In his extremely influential work *The Spirit of the Laws*, Montesquieu (1748) made one error that was to have a great impact on subsequent constitutional theorising. Because of his own monarchist allegiance, Montesquieu was insufficiently sensitive to the consequences of the 'Glorious Revolution' of the previous century. He thus confused the formalities with the realities and placed the monarch at the head of the Executive—one of his three divisions of government.[1] Had he been more fully aware of the real distribution of power in the eighteenth-century British regime, he might have paid closer attention to the role of the head of state, as distinguished from that of the real head of government.

When the American founding fathers came to adapt the Montesquieu framework for a new republic, they were content to replace what they believed to have

---

1   Although Montesquieu did not use the term 'branch', it has consistently appeared in glosses on the US constitution, with consequences that I consider to have been significant. I thus disagree with Rohr (1995:39), who considers the modern preference for the term (over, for example, the previously favoured 'department') as being little more than a change in fashion. In this case, I contend, the term 'branch' does carry important connotations, for it can be used—in ways seemingly not open to other terms—to legitimise hegemony over a major sector of modern governance. The establishment of this hegemony could initially have been due to its very trinitarian structure. After rejecting a seventeenth-century view that the durability of this structure was due to its having 'shadowed' the structure of the Christian deity, Vile (1967:15) immediately goes on to remark on the 'mystical' quality it has acquired. I have not yet been able to determine how this terminology came to be dominant. The *Oxford English Dictionary* cites the earliest use of the term in the early eighteenth century. In 1712, in *The Spectator* (no. 287), Joseph Addison wrote that ancient sages such as Polybius and Cicero 'gave the Pre-eminence to a mixt Government, consisting of three Branches, the Regal, the Noble, and the Popular'. Addison went on to warn that 'a greater number (than four Branches) would cause too much confusion'. We need the services of an intellectual historian of the skill of Hirschman to chart the evolution of this term. Some time ago, much of the relevant material was gathered by Vile (1967), except he, like Rohr, was insufficiently aware of the political weight that accrues to interests once they have succeeded in laying claim to the rubric of 'branch'. He does, however, at one point draw attention to the need to consider closely—as no less a thinker than Locke had done under the rubric of a 'federative' function—the attractiveness of another branch: 'Locke and others had been bothered by the fact that the "ruler"...had to carry out the law when it was clear and easily stated, principally in internal affairs, but he had also to act in areas where the law could not be laid down in detail and where his prerogative must remain almost wholly untrammeled, that is to say largely in external affairs. Thus between them Locke and Montesquieu state at least *four* functions of government, not three: the legislative, the executive, the "prerogative", and the judicial' (Vile 1967:87). In this monograph, I am contending that this prerogative power be revived under the aegis of the head of state, and broadened in scope, so as to serve a monitory function.

been an executive monarchy with an executive president. As Vile (1967:121) has pointed out, this was all too easy for them to do, for the colonial governors, with whom most of them had tangled, possessed powers close to those that Montesquieu had falsely attributed to the monarch. From its inception in this way, the head-of-state role in the United States has been subordinated to that of the head of government, which has in turn become determined by the outcomes of partisan elections. So much for the independence of the head of state in presidential regimes.

In the other form of regime that came to prominence in the twentieth century— the parliamentarist—the threefold Montesquieu differentiation of branches has come to be adopted uncritically, except that it has always been apparent to those involved in these regimes that the head of state could no longer be considered the head of government. As a result, only a small space could be found in the Montesquieu trinity for the head of state. Heads of state in parliamentarist regimes might have become more independent of partisan politics than they have been in presidential regimes, but they have done so at the cost of marginalisation. At no point has the question been posed: should the head of state be accorded the status of playing a leading role in a separate branch of governance?

c) On fiducial governance

It will by now be apparent that if I am to take up the Geertzian challenge in the context of Australian republicanism, I shall have to work out of 'left field', for the mainstream has become stalled by Montesquieu orthodoxies; hence my resort to a near-neologism in the very title of this monograph. By 'fiducial governance', I mean a commitment by our nation-state to adopt policies and arrange institutional relations in ways that demonstrably strengthen the trust of the citizenry in its institutions of governance. If this commitment is made and followed through, it will end up generating a strong—indeed, in my view, ultimately irresistible—movement to a republican order in Australia.

Composing this monograph out of left field will inevitably open me to charges of elitism, in the sense that I shall at some key points be directing complex arguments at governance elites. Such an orientation cannot be avoided, however, as I am seeking to encourage a substantial change in the culture of constitutional reform in Australia. I am seeking to remedy a state of affairs that has been described by Irving (2009:118): 'The republic campaign generated a body of theoretical work, but did not engage deeply with questions of constitutionalism. The bill of rights issue looks likely to be similar. The focus in such themes has tended to be practical, rather than conceptual or analytical.'

In order to do this, I am exploring some important structural changes to our current machinery of government arrangements—to provide institutional room, as it were, for governance practitioners to begin the work that will produce the needed cultural transformations. Only when these changes—both cultural and structural—have been effected will it be possible for political activists, with skills I do not possess, to craft proposals for concrete changes that will stand good chances of popular approval through a referendum.

A genuine government commitment to fiducial governance will result in a wide-ranging reform program; there are serious problems that require attention and the very process of implementing reforms will in time make it easier to secure public approval in a public referendum on constitutional changes. As the late former Senator David Hamer—that shrewd political practitioner—observed about the most promising way of achieving constitutional reform in the Australian system:

> If…there could be a working period with the new rules before there was any need to include the rules in the various constitutions, by this time they would be accepted practice, and the conservatism of the voters on constitutional matters would be recruited on the side of their acceptance. (Hamer 1994:83)

The character of this monograph is therefore tentative and contingent in tone. It is too early to make confident judgments about the nature of the constitutional reforms that might ultimately be needed. It is possible, however, to outline a framework within which new collegial bodies can begin the needed work without any prior constitutional recognition.

There are important further dimensions to fiducial governance than just the advancement of the trustworthiness of public institutions—vital as that might be. Often, the most effective way forward is to follow the famous injunction of Braithwaite (1998): 'Institutionalise distrust; enculture trust.' For this reason, it is of the utmost importance for regime stability that new institutional arrangements (whether they be for the establishment—in recent times, strongly advocated—of an integrity branch, or, as I would prefer it to be titled, a monitory branch) be designed in ways that prevent corruption before it occurs (Brown 2008:46). And, if this is to occur, the trust that underpins fiducial governance must be especially strong between those officials who are heading up the several monitory units that are being brought together in the new branch.

The term 'fiducial' has close connections with other terms in wider use, such as 'consensual' and 'consociational'.[2] 'Fiducial', however, can be differentiated

---

2   The term derives from the cognate Latin term '*fides*' (trust) and has until now not been used in governance contexts, its current use being restricted largely to physics and theology. It is thus free of the legal and sometimes confusing connotations of the more familiar term 'fiduciary'.

from the others because of its emphasis on the close interrelations between leaders and the citizenry. All such terms are readily distinguishable from that which is most commonly used to describe democratic politics: the 'partisan'. Parties lie at the heart of modern representative democracies, but parties alone cannot deliver good governance. Party politicians often engage in politics other than the partisan; much of the time of many parliamentarians is devoted to non-partisan committee work (Halligan et al. 2007:ch.8). The distinctive feature of such contemporary fiducial politics when it is compared with the partisan form is, however, its fragmented and largely unorganised nature. It is this relative lack of coherence that has determined the lack of success to date of calls for the recognition of an integrity branch—that is, a formation that in my terms would focus primarily on fiducial politics. As I shall argue, the boundaries between the two forms of politics would be best determined on a case-by-case basis by the members of high-level collegial bodies, of which a majority would be members of political parties, but they would be partisans who recognised the need to collaborate across party lines with others with strong fiducial commitments.

The reach of fiducial politics therefore extends well beyond the domain of political leader–citizen relations, for it must affect the ways in which politicians themselves relate to each other. As it does this, it can also lead to a long-overdue rejuvenation of the parties themselves. As increasing numbers of citizens come to see the opportunities for participation in meaningful discourse about the major issues of the day, they will be attracted to parties that offer them the most effective ways of so participating.

Anticipating much of the argument that follows, Table P.1 indicates one way in which this could be done. Fiducial governance, I shall be contending, is most likely when a separate branch is dedicated to the tasks of making public policies worthy of the trust of the citizenry, and a monitory branch is well suited to such tasks.

Table P.1 A possible fourth branch of the State differentiated from the familiar three

		Principal political considerations on peak collegial body (shown in each case in parentheses)	
		Partisan	Non-partisan
Principal style of branch structuring in order to relate to interests in civil society	Hierarchical	Executive (Cabinet)	Judicial (High Court)
	Reciprocal (through elections and committee inquiries)	Legislative (Parliament)	Monitory (Council of State)

So what are the serious problems that need urgent attention because they have been diminishing public trust in our institutions of governance? I begin the first section of this monograph by addressing this critical question.

Introduction

a) The need for reform

I can most readily provide a simple introduction to what is wrong with the current Australian system of governance by listing 10 excellent modern works that have called for needed changes in our regime but that seem for the most part to have been going nowhere

- *Report* of the Review of Public Service Personnel Management in Victoria (1990)
- *Report* of the Republic Advisory Committee (1993)
- *Can Responsible Government Survive in Australia?* (Hamer 1994)
- *The Road to a Republic* (Parliament of Australia 2004)
- *Into the Future: The neglect of the long term in Australian politics* (Marsh and Yencken 2004)
- *Chaos or Coherence: Strengths, opportunities and challenges for Australia's integrity systems – the NISA Report* (Griffith University Institute for Ethics, Governance and Law and Transparency International 2005)
- *An Australian Republic* (Barns and Krawec-Wheaton 2006)
- *Restraining Elective Dictatorship: The upper house solution?* (Aroney et al. 2008)
- *Promoting Integrity: Evaluating and improving public institutions* (Head et al. 2008)
- *National Human Rights Consultation Report* (Australian Human Rights Commission 2009a)
- *Choosing the Republic* (Patmore 2009)

It is not easy to trace the reasons why these numerous recommendations, which I for the most part support and find progressive, have been stalled. Nevertheless, the *Into the Future* essay most readily provides us with several of the most salient reasons for its own lack of impact—reasons that are relevant to the others as well. Chief among these is the continuing dominance of our highly disciplined political parties, which have tightened their hold on the levers of power as their community bases have dwindled. The continuing dominance of the parties means that the institution on which Marsh and Yencken pin their hopes—the Parliament[1]—cannot assume the position of centrality envisaged for it by them as long as the party system remains unchanged.

In the assumptive world of Marsh and Yencken, there is no other institution available to impose new disciplines on the parties that for so long have imposed their own forms of narrow disciplines on policymaking leaders, including those in the Parliament itself. To anticipate a central theme in this monograph, however: what of a directly elected head of state, seated in a council of state in which all the familiar branches of governance were represented? Like all those who have concerned themselves with public policymaking in modern Australia, Marsh and Yencken do not consider this possibility.

There has in recent years been some valuable work done by such entities as Transparency International and its Australian partners (for example, Griffith University 2005; Head et al. 2008). The character of this work has, however, been insufficiently political in nature; the proponents of the cause seeking the establishment in each of our jurisdictions of an integrity branch have not seriously addressed the questions of how structural reforms could generate the political support needed for the implementation of their reform proposals. Such political support could be developed around the ideal of fiduciality in governance—the development of a system that would heighten citizen trust in governance while simultaneously not threatening the legitimacy of the policy priorities of the government of the day. So we must next examine more closely the need for fiduciality, before going on to explore the reasons why the considerations raised by this concept have been so little considered in debates about our republican future.

The citizenry of Australia, like its counterparts in other similar societies, displays a constantly low level of trust in its public institutions (Bean 2005:123–4).

Accordingly, the most careful recent examination of the state of our democracy has concluded that the Australian public exhibits 'disengagement and lack of trust in existing representative institutions, from political parties through to NGOs' (Sawer et al. 2009:246). Unsurprisingly, then, Australia has not escaped the international trend that has witnessed the steady diminution of the membership of the major parties (Sawer et al. 2009:136). And most recent surveys show that the majority of Australians do not trust the institutions of government (Sawer et al. 2009:149), and an even higher majority believes corruption to be unacceptably high, especially in large private sector firms.

---

1   In their essay, Marsh and Yencken cite seven overseas institutional initiatives relevant to their concerns. Of these, no fewer than five are parliamentary.

Associated with these 'disturbing trends' has been a lack of public confidence in the capacity of the legal system to remedy these defects (Braithwaite 2008:185; Sawer et al. 2009:41).

What is most disturbing about this state of affairs has been the spread of distrust, so that it extends to all the participants—government and non-government—that have become involved in modern governance.[2] Reform policies that are aimed only at government institutions will not therefore be sufficient; fiducial policies and programs must cover the full range of governance institutions—public and private.

b) Opening up the assumptive world of the republican policy community

Every policy community has its assumptive world—a set of interlocking and usually unquestioned assumptions that together help it make some sort of sense of the policy domain with which it is concerned. Despite this commonality, policy communities differ in terms of the scope of their concerns: the more narrowly drawn the boundaries around its domain, the tighter are likely to be the sets of assumptions that bind together the participants in that community. Although I shall be arguing that the republican *spirit* should be one that is constantly questioning assumptions and imputations, in Australia, the republican policy community has been bound tightly by the assumptions of its core agency: the Australian Republican Movement (ARM).[3]

In subjecting these assumptions to critical scrutiny, I am not making assumptions of my own about their invalidity. Some of the assumptions made by mainstream republicans could turn out to be well grounded. For example, the assumption that the two head-of-state offices that currently serve us could conveniently be merged into one office *could* end up being the arrangement that finally comes into being. I doubt that it will, but deliberations in one or other of the councils of state—whose creation I shall be recommending—might produce agreement on a merged head-of-state office. So, while I am not contending that all that is

---

2   Indeed, the two least-trusted sets of institutions are, according to Bean (2005:Table 8.3), non-governmental: banks and financial institutions and trade unions.

3   Because the domain of the policy community has been so tightly drawn, the ARM has been dominant, in a way that it would not have been had the relevant policy community been one that concerned itself with broader issues of constitutional reform. This dominance has been so pronounced that I have recently felt free to describe it as 'colonising' other nearby formations (Power 2008b). Responding to an earlier draft of this monograph, one of the readers, who himself had been a leader of the ARM, commented that its strategy had been supported by '99% of the wider republican movement, including the Australian Labor Party, the Australian Democrats and the Australian Greens. ARM is not alone in wanting to move directly towards a republic'. Exactly!

contained in the assumptive worlds of those in the mainstream of contemporary republicans is wrong, I am contending that stronger republican thinking is needed. Rather than an ossified republican policy community, we need a strongly republican approach to constitutional reform—an approach that was sadly absent in the 1990s.

In Australia, the republican policy community was to a significant extent the initiative of the Prime Minister of the day, Paul Keating. He took advantage of the then recent creation of the ARM to attempt to build a policy community around it, led by the then leader of the ARM, Malcolm Turnbull, whom he appointed to chair an advisory committee on how to proceed towards the republic. Turnbull was quite open about his lack of interest in comparative and philosophical issues: 'a gram of Australian experience is worth…a tonne of experience in other countries' (Turnbull 1993:114). In practice, Turnbull was even more blinkered than this, for he did not accord overseas experience even a gram of weight in his recommendations. And further, he did not really accord any more weight to sub-national experiences in Australia itself.

Right from the start, the fundamental problem was that the issues raised by the transition to a republic were of themselves of interest to only a small minority. Unless these issues could be tied into issues of greater public resonance, opponents of change could cast the proponents as elitists. As things turned out, this monarchist tactic was quite effective.

While any constitutional reformer must always be alive to political pragmatics, the approach adopted at any one time will be very much a product of the governance climate of that time. And here Turnbull was out of luck, for the leader who gave the republican cause such momentum was Keating, and his approach to political pragmatics was not appropriate for the republican project. Keating and his coterie gained an unenviable reputation for arrogant, top-down styles of policymaking. Consider this characterisation of the style from one of Keating's insiders (with not a hint of embarrassment about its hubris):

> Working Nation created the desire to do more. If it was possible to conceive of the means to case-manage tens of thousands of young unemployed, it was possible to case-manage regions and communities. If it was possible to re-imagine the way governments dealt with unemployment, it was possible to re-imagine the way they dealt with Aboriginal health. If the government could take on the challenge of the revolution in business and industry, it could take on the revolution in technology. If it could do these things, surely it might raise the level of knowledge and interest in the democracy itself—in its institutions, the ideas from which they derived, in the nation's history. We could move on to civics and education generally. (Watson 2002:491)

Turnbull and *his* insiders apparently did not find this style all that inimical, for they too believed they had the answers before they ventured into the public domain. Here is the account of the Republic Advisory Committee's public consultations in Perth from John Hirst, a noted historian, ARM leader and member of the committee:

> All round the country professors of politics are indignant. The republican movement has taken off without waiting to listen to their lectures on the true nature of republicanism…
>
> One professor, after finishing his polished address, was about to resume his seat when [chairman] Turnbull, switching into lawyer mode, said: 'One moment, please professor. Would you return to the witness box for cross-examination?' In twenty seconds Turnbull had him making concessions and retractions which undid the force of his paper. (Hirst 1994:28)

The accuracy of this account has been challenged by one of the politics professors present at the hearing in question (O'Brien 1995:56). What is of primary relevance here, however, is not the accuracy of Hirst's account, but rather its extraordinary endorsement of the inappropriate behaviour of his chairman. It is not the job of the chairman of a public inquiry to harass witnesses and it was an abuse of Turnbull's position for him to have done so. The most likely explanation for Turnbull's behaviour—and for Hirst's uncritical endorsement of it—is that the ARM leaders had already decided, in 'group-think' fashion, what they were going to recommend, so public hearings were a waste of time. This of course turned out to be a self-fulfilling prophecy, for the hearings *were* a failure—one that greatly weakened the republican cause. In the public mind, this cause came to be perceived as another exercise in haughty Keating elitism.

From this extremely top-down perspective on policymaking, all that was needed to solve any problem was the getting together of a small number of the Keating cognoscenti, for they believed that they had between them discovered the magic technique of successful policy development. It turned out, however, that the one thing they had not discovered was a way of avoiding a landslide defeat in the next election. As long as the Keating government remained in office, however, it seemed that insiders such as Hirst could be brought to depart from their normal academic disciplines if they believed that they had come up with simple solutions to complex problems. And their shared belief could be summed up in one word: minimalism.

The most serious of the several assumptions of the Australian republican policy community has been that which denies a significant continuing political role for the head of state. Because of this denial, the policy community has found it convenient to develop a minimalist strategy. If the Australian public could be persuaded that the constitutional changes proposed were only minor ones, it seemed to believe, perhaps it would be possible to sneak a referendum affirmation through, 'on the quiet', as it were.

The fatal flaw in this strategy became apparent in the referendum campaign. The monarchists found common ground with some of the leaders of the direct-electionist republicans;[4] both saw much more substance in the head-of-state role than did the minimalists. Unless the positive contributions that monarchs have made to the quality of Australian governance are acknowledged and learned from, a way out of this impasse will not be found[5].

Good as the Australian system of government has been, it has—in keeping with all the other national regimes around the world—been less sure as it has sought to handle the emerging system of governance. While government lies and should lie at the core of governance in any nation, the emerging system must also attend to non-governmental institutions that have come to prominence in an age of privatisation and outsourcing. Australia confronts a historic opportunity as we move into the new millennium. Just as our colonies took many leads in democratisation in the nineteenth century, the transition to a republic could lead Australia to an important reorientation of political activity, to make it more suited to many of the tasks now beginning to press insistently on national governments around the globe.

c) Beyond minimalism

It will be the central proposition of this monograph that the State and its head must be accorded a leadership role in the pursuit of truly republican governance, but this proposition can be developed only in a broad systemic context. We need to fashion a comprehensive and internally coherent framework of republican governance—one that recognises the strengths, and remedies the weaknesses, of our current arrangements. By establishing this broad context, we can examine the ways in which any reforms that might be proposed to deal with weaknesses in one element might unintentionally affect other elements, and go on to propose ways in which undesirable effects might be avoided.[6]

---

4   No wonder some of the direct electionists found common cause with the monarchists, for they were scorned by the leaders of the republican policy community. They reminded Malcolm Turnbull (1999:2) 'of Reformation fanatics burning heretics at the stake to save their souls'.

5   In making this assertion, I subscribe to a long-forgotten Australian tradition, recently recovered by Cochrane (2006: 535 n.301), in his characterisation of John Dunmore Lang as a 'loyal republican', who only came to adopt a republican stance when monarchical arrangements had proved lacking.

6   Beer (1973:76 ff.) has proposed a term—'*engrenage*'—to cover a familiar phenomenon: the ways in which government attempts to deal with problems themselves lead to new problems.

We are entering an age in which many of the established boundaries—between, say, law and convention or between the public and the private sectors—are becoming blurred. Democratic government is an essential part of any approach to this blurring phenomenon, but it cannot do it all itself. A new form of politics—to exist alongside partisan politics—needs to be formally recognised and needs to work through a new form of institution, one that reconciles the demands of democracy with those of fiducial republican governance. I shall be arguing that this new form of institution will be councils of state, sitting at the head of equally new monitory branches.

Although I voted in favour of the republican proposal put to the Australian people a decade ago, I am now glad that the proposal was defeated. Too much of the work needed on constitutional reform remained—and still remains!—to be done. Why has this necessary work remained undone?

In the 1990s, the work was not done because of the imminence of the new millennium. It was felt by those leading the republican charge—most notably, Keating and Turnbull—that there was no time to waste if the window of opportunity that they believed to be presented by the centenary of federation were to be used. Although they therefore favoured a minimalist approach, so that all considerations except those suggested by commonsense as being relevant to the abolition of the monarchy were set aside, the intensity of their campaign had a 'crowding out' effect. No other constitutional reform proposals have come to centre stage during or since the republican campaign, which has made the past two decades the most bereft of deliberations on such matters in the entire history of the Australian nation. Why has this emptiness continued over the past decade, since the defeat of the republican referendum?

Part of the explanation for this sad state of affairs must go to the quality of leadership provided by Prime Minister John Howard, who must surely have been the political leader least interested in constitutional reform of any that Australia has experienced.[7] The reasons, however, go deeper than this. The minimalism so favoured by Keating and Turnbull in the 1990s has continued to blight deliberations on both the republic and wider issues of constitutional reform.

Yet, some valuable work was done within the minimalist paradigm, and this work can be used to provide relevant launching pads for wider-ranging considerations of the nature of the republic that will be needed in the years ahead. Only when we come to the end of this long journey will it be time for a further referendum on the transition to a fully republican state. This journey will be a long one because the minimalist paradigm will not be easy to shift; it is

---

7   According to Ahamed and Davis (2009:222), this Howard diffidence about structural reform extended so widely that they could claim that 'public sector reform was not a key policy interest of the Howard years'.

deeply embedded in the commonsense so close to the hearts of most fashioners of public policies in Australia. But shift it will, quite possibly only after another defeat—this time of a premature plebiscite proposal[8]—has demonstrated the dead-end nature of the minimalist paradigm.

So lengthy will this period of reorientation have to be that I have now come to the realisation that I shall not see a fully republican Australia in my lifetime. Somewhat to my surprise, this realisation has served to free me up to begin the work of directly confronting the minimalist paradigm—a task that has to date confounded me. To know that I need only make a start, and that future generations will finally come to benefit from the constitutional reforms (that might have to await the demise of the minimalist paradigm), has turned out to be liberating.[9]

Counter-posing this sense of liberation is a realisation that reforms of the magnitude that are needed will carry appreciable risks of regime malfunctioning. I have attempted to minimise these risks by placing collegial bodies—made up of the most experienced governance practitioners—at the centre of the proposed new regime. In an important sense they will be performing the tasks that have been those discharged by those once dubbed (in more sexist times) 'founding fathers'. Such collegial bodies should be relied on to cope with unexpected but sometimes serious problems as they arise.

Writing about the American founding fathers, Davis (1995:27–8) made an insightful observation that applies more widely to numerous other constitutional enterprises: 'they had composed a new form of government with no precise, no defined, no known principles of action. But at base, experience would have told them that as a people conducts its politics, so it gives content to its institutions and its principles.'

---

8   In 2008, the Leader of the Greens, Senator Bob Brown, introduced into the Parliament a bill to require the government to hold such a plebiscite at the time of the 2010 general election. Fortunately, this will not happen. In June 2009, the Senate Committee on Finance and Public Administration reported that the bill should not be supported during the life of the current Parliament. (This was about the only merit of the extremely limp report of the committee. Anyone wishing to see a recent example of the aimlessness of current republican thinking in Australia could do no better than to examine this superficial report: Parliament of Australia 2009a.)

9   In a recent essay reviewing my life's work, I have come to the sad conclusion that it has had little continuing effect on the work of others (Power 2009). Perhaps this suggests an answer to the curiously liberating effect that this project has had; in this case, I cannot know in my lifetime whether this essay will be different from those that have preceded it, so I can hope that it might ultimately come to exert some influence.

d) Governance and the State

Both governance and the State are concerned with what Low and Power (1984) termed the 'APRA': the aggregate of policy-relevant activities. Many of these activities—usually the most important of them—are either determined or shaped by governments, but several are not. Whether they are so shaped or not, all the activities in the APRA that fall within its prescribed geographical area of sovereignty are the concern of the modern State. The domain of the nation-state is thus much wider than that of the government that is embedded in it.

There is therefore a close correspondence (at least for the purposes of this monograph) between national governance, on the one hand, and the concerns of modern states and their heads, on the other. Of course, in the current era of globalisation, many governance activities are not shaped by the modern State; in the memorable term of Rosenau (1992), in many international fields, we now have governance without government. Although this condition of affairs should concern the democrat, it has generally been considered that it could not be remedied in the absence of world government, and the governments of existing nation-states would never tolerate such a regime. In an epilogue to a companion essay to this monograph, I briefly consider the ways in which national councils of state might come together to form a global council of states in a way that might not be opposed by the governments of the world.

e) Energising our publics

When Australia finally does make it to a republic, such a change will be worthy of the appellation 'constitutional moment'—probably only the third, after the advent of responsible government a century and a half ago and federation a half-century later, in the whole history of white settlement of the continent. A constitutional moment is one when significant shift occurs in the balance of established powers.

Ackerman, who introduced the term in order to come to gain a handle on the achievements of three of the greatest US presidents to date—Thomas Jefferson, Abraham Lincoln and Franklin Roosevelt—used it to refer to great accretions of presidential power, in the last resort independently of what the formal provisions of the nation's constitution might have stated (Ackerman 1998:409).[10] Of course, the dramatic contexts of these three 'moments'—nation building, civil war and the Great Depression—provided these skilled politicians with openings not normally available to political leaders. How could the advent of a republic in Australia ever provide a context even remotely like these?

If we are to attempt an answer to this central question, we must identify a set of issues with the potential power to energise the Australian citizenry. This will be harder to do than in the two earlier constitutional moments in Australia, because the nature of the citizenry has changed so radically. Our culture no longer possesses the heavily 'British' deferential culture that supported our political leaders in their earlier achievements.[11] And our party system is now in an enervated state, with our party grassroots populated largely by those hoping to gain some office through party backing. This sad condition of our parties has not, however, inhibited them in the accumulation of ever-greater power. They are indeed well described in the epithet 'hypertrophied' (that is, overextended).

Some party leaders—for obvious reasons usually those who have retired (most notably, the late John Button and Malcolm Fraser)—have protested about the directions in which their parties have been heading. The parties will be regenerated, however, only when they come to support a broad movement—a 'fiducial' movement—towards the fostering of institutional integrity for our major institutions. Of course, this movement will not—initially at least—be one that will attract deep popular support. We now have the tools, however—if our political leaders so wish—to build the needed momentum.

f) Trust and government

So, what can governments do to promote the cause of fiducial governance? There are, after all, persuasive grounds for contending that often it is governments themselves that are predators on community-based trust: 'Over the last five thousand years, most people across the world have relied on trust networks for these (high-risk) enterprises, and have guarded the responsible networks as much as possible from governmental intervention' (Tilly 2005:43).

---

10   In Ackerman's view, these moments have been rare in American history, for 'a constitutional moment need not ripen into a new constitutional solution' (Ackerman 1998:409). This conception of the 'constitutional moment' is particularly stimulating when we come to consider the ways in which this insight might be used in the design of a future 'moment'. As I shall argue below, a regime that separated the roles of head of state and head of government, and that possessed a collegial body (such as a council of state or a French-style constitutional council to be consulted on relations between the two) (Rohr 1995:22–3, 48 ff.), could offer a more congenial institutional setting than the American system for the workings of a fiducial republican order.
11   Of course, some of the more optimistic of the republicans have contended that the transition to a republic might itself have an energising effect (Uhr 1999:3).

Australia's most famous corruption fighter, Tony Fitzgerald, has recently provided yet another perspective that illustrates the difficulty of reform. As Fitzgerald (2010) observes, political leaders themselves serve as role models, and if their behaviour is deficient, a vicious circle ensues: 'People who consider themselves powerless outsiders readily become disillusioned, cynical, apathetic and disengaged and lose trust in government, the integrity of its process and decisions and even fundamental institutions. Principled leadership is essential to preserve our confidence in and support for each other.'

So there should be no doubt as to the extreme difficulty of this task. And the best account of this difficulty is that of Tilly (2005). Central to Tilly's analysis is the trust network, which he defines tightly as the formation into which people set valued resources that have been placed at risk, typically from the mistakes and failures of others. In this way, he hopes to avoid the vagueness that so often engulfs discussions of the relationships between trust and democratisation (such as the *glissandi* that he plausibly ascribes to the well-known work of Putnam).

Useful as this analytical category is for Tilly, it ultimately is not as relevant as it might have been for the task that has been set for this monograph. Tilly adopts as his primary perspective the interests embedded in his trust networks. From this perspective, governments are seen as dangerous, because 'regimes and trust networks often depend on the same resources—labor, power, money, information, loyalty, and more' (Tilly 2005:23).

Dangerous as governments might be, Tilly does recognise some instances— relatively rare ones, in his view—when trust networks can be satisfactorily integrated into 'public politics'. At no point, however, does Tilly recognise the potential value of a differing perspective—one that accords primacy to a head of state in fostering trust among the citizenry.

It is my contention[12] that the decline in the authority and power of monarchical heads of state has been an important cause of this loss of state capacity. Therefore, I propose that a strategy to invest new resources in a reinvigorated office of head of state should be able to recapture some of the public trust that has been lost. The opportunity exists for a nation such as Australia, which has been struggling to find a way through to a republic, to do so in ways that further the cause of fiducial governance.

---

12   At present, this can be no more than a contention, for the decline of heads of states everywhere preceded the advent of public opinion surveys. It is now nearly a century since the collapse of many monarchies during and immediately after World War I. Experience in the interwar years—especially the accession of Adolf Hitler to the office of German head of state—greatly fostered suspicion of the office. In the past decade or so, however, the emergence of semi-presidential regimes has reconfigured some head-of-state roles so as to invest them with moderate substantive powers. As we shall shortly see, that should be enough for current reform purposes.

1. A framework for constitutional reform

a) The contingent nature of this monograph

The basic principle that should underlie any attempt at constitutional reform is one that is fundamentally Old Institutionalist in character (Power 2009) and, possibly because of this, the need for caution often seems better appreciated by the citizenry than by the experts; any change must safeguard those arrangements that time has shown to have worked well.[1] For the most part, the Australian system of government has performed as well as most democracies, so we should be especially careful when we consider changing it.

If we are to move towards a new regime, we need to be clear about the distinction between the monarchical and the republican styles of governance. The former is quite comfortable with the buried and the implicit; the latter is always engaged in the Sisyphean tasks of making explicit what can be made so, of always holding open to question crucial assumptions whenever they are discovered.[2]

In this monograph, then, I shall be aiming to demonstrate how the existing Australian governance regime could be modified in ways that would be of international significance.

To date, progress towards a republic in Australia has been blocked by a deep division between the direct electionists and the selectionists. This division will continue as long as the two schools of opinion see themselves competing for the definition of a single office of head of state and the way that person

---

1   Shklar (1987:60) has presented a salutary Montesquieuian caution at this point: 'tampering with a long-established system…is always a very dangerous thing to do. For it is only in retrospect that we can recognize what the basis of its stability was.' Sometimes, however, circumstances demand reform; all that those who undertake such reform can do is to be as conscious as they can be of the strengths that the old system exhibited.
2   This characterisation of the republican style of governance might seem to be at variance with the Montesquieuian position, at least as this has been put by Shklar (1987:78–9): 'Republican constitutions are exceptionally fragile because they depend on the customs, habits and attitudes of the citizens.' A Burkean might well ask why this should make such regimes so fragile. The important point to be made in the current context is, however, that the English regime that Montesquieu extolled worked well because the monarchy delivered the public trust needed. Weaken the monarchy—as has happened in Australia—and more explicit attention must be paid to the fashioning of public trust through fiducial arrangements.

should be selected.[3] Progress to the republic will resume when it comes to be widely recognised that what the two schools want might be so different as to warrant a continuation of the current bicephalous arrangement: a monarch (to be replaced by an elected president) and a set of governors (left largely, but far from completely, undisturbed).

b) Towards a feasible framework

Somewhat later in this section, it will become apparent that, in preparing the theoretical framework for this monograph, I have drawn most from the recent works of two scholars: Bruce Ackerman and John Keane. At the outset, however, I want to make one observation about these two writers that sets the scene for all that is to follow in this section. I have been encouraged by the preparedness of both writers to go beyond the Rhodes observation at the head of this monograph and propose that new good governance regimes—constrained parliamentarianism and monitory democracy—could be acknowledged in ways that accommodated the numerous institutional mechanisms (estimated by Keane to number close to 100) that now constrain our governments.

Between them, however, Ackerman and Keane did not take me far enough in probing some of the machinery of government issues that will need to be settled before we can progress to a regime of fiducial governance. Neither of them has attended to the emergent roles that heads of state could play in such a new regime, so neither of them has gone on to consider the ways in which the emergence of such roles could greatly strengthen the reform of constitutional monarchies along republican lines.

Now, because the exploration of several of these theoretical concerns will take me well into the left field noted by my two readers, it would be likely to turn off many of the Australian readers with republican interests. Accordingly, I am preparing two works—one theoretical and comparative (Power forthcoming), and this one—in which several of the theoretical points made in the first piece will be presented as givens in the development of the more practically oriented argument of this monograph.[4]

---

3   The project that has produced this monograph had its roots in the 1990s, when Australians were confronted with the opportunity of moving on from the monarchist regime that had so well served the interests of European Australians for a couple of centuries. Our reluctance to take that opportunity, on the terms in which it was presented in a referendum, has convinced me that an Australian republic will be worth having only if it opens up the prospects for better governance. Determining just how republicanism and good governance are best related has for me proven to be a daunting task—and one on which I have only now embarked.

4   In the fullness of time, interested readers will be able to access the theoretical arguments in full in the companion essay. If, however, the appearance of this companion essay occurs only some months after the appearance of this monograph, a stopgap arrangement will be required. Anyone wishing to obtain a draft copy of my theoretical essay—or any of the other unpublished papers of mine listed in the references—can

c) Writing about fiducial governance: two constituencies

I identify two differing constituencies of readers from whom intelligence will be needed if the necessary governance design work is to be satisfactorily progressed. This design work will be far beyond the capacity of a single individual and will require substantial inputs from knowledgeable constituencies. All that this individual will be able to do is to propose some frameworks for the organisation of varied forms of intelligence as they come in.

The first constituency—and the one at which a companion essay is being aimed (Power forthcoming)—is that of the comparative administrationists, for one of my primary concerns is the exploration of some fundamental issues concerned with machinery of government matters. In particular, I wish in that essay to explore in some depth questions about the ways in which the branches of governance have been conceptualised and differentiated.

The second constituency—and the one at which this monograph is aimed—is that of governance practitioners in a nation-state that impresses me as being exceptionally well placed to lead in the introduction of a new fiducial governance regime: the Commonwealth of Australia. While the argument in this monograph will be informed by several of the findings of the more theoretical companion essay, it will not probe as deeply, for many of the working premises of the Australian machinery of government will be taken as givens.

In this way, I hope that knowledgeable members of these two constituencies will be able to provide us with the intelligence we shall need if we are to progress to a fuller appreciation of the nature of fiducial governance regimes in the twenty-first century. If the interpretative framework I shall be presenting gains some acceptance, it could be possible to compose a series of collaborative monographs on the reforms of particular regimes and, indeed, of global institutions as well.

I shall be contending that we shall realise the promise of fiducial governance only if we explicitly recognise that the leading roles in such governance are highly political. The constitutional design task is not politically to neuter our heads of state, but rather to consider ways in which these political roles can be reconciled with the needs of democratic government.

This will not be an easy design task, for the twentieth century witnessed the steady erosion of the traditional head-of-state roles that had earlier protected

---

obtain copies from me: <john.power@unimelb.edu.au> In addition, although they have not been listed in the references, I have been publishing in *The Australian Journal of Public Administration* a set of reviews of several of the works that are listed in the references: Boyce (June 2009), Head et al. (December 2009), Patmore (March 2010), Keane (June 2010) and Kumarasingham (September 2010).

the integrity of each nation's major institutions. The vacuum so created has produced growing anxiety about the effectiveness of the mechanisms that are now in place to counter corruption and protect institutional integrity. So strong have these concerns shown themselves to be that there has in recent times been increasing support for the recognition of new 'integrity branches' of government, but to date no-one has proposed that revived heads of state could be accorded leadership positions in such branches.

In pre-democratic times, heads of state typically played central roles in governance. Because most of these heads of state were monarchs, modern democratic theory has universally marginalised them, so that these traditional roles have fallen into desuetude.

Accordingly, both presidents and constitutional monarchs have been largely ignored in recent discussions about the nature of modern governance. As a result, insufficient attention has been paid to some serious issues concerned with the maintenance of public responsibility for the quality of our governance. Because discussion of possible head-of-state roles has been taboo, no-one has yet given serious attention to the overall design of the branch structures of governance and the ways in which they could be accommodated in existing machineries of government. There is thus a significant gap in our understanding of fiducial governance.

Anyone doubting the existence of this serious gap in our understanding of governance need go no further than Fukuyama's seminal work, *Trust: The social virtues and the creation of prosperity* (1995).

The argument that sustains the work is both stimulating and subtle and provides us with much of what we need as we go about the task of specifying a meaning for fiducial governance. Yet, Fukuyama himself does not use his own materials in this way. Although he remarks in passing (on p. 355) that the phenomenon of trust is probably more central to the political than to the economic sphere, his work—as its subtitle indicates—remains oriented much more to the latter than to the former.

As Fukuyama convincingly argues, much of the content of trust cannot be legislated, for its existence depends on informal but generally recognised rules—what (although Fukuyama himself does not mention it) in constitutional studies are termed conventions.

One of the most intriguing of the patterns uncovered by Fukuyama is the apparent link between constitutional monarchy and relatively high levels of trust. On the measure central to his analysis—the capacity of a nation to foster the emergence of a multinational firm—constitutional monarchies (Japan, Britain, Sweden and the Netherlands) have loomed large. If Australia is to proceed to a republican regime, great care will be needed if the positive features of constitutional monarchies are not to be disrupted. Yet the republican policy community in Australia has been strangely unconcerned about this need. If we are to progress further down the pathway to a republic, we need to understand the reasons for this neglect, so as to be able to transcend it.

d) Regaining the sacred at the centre of governance

> [T]he sense of the sacred is allowed to erode. Everything in public life risks being desacralized: persons, places, pledges, prayers, practices, words, sacred writings, religious formulas, symbols, ceremonies.
>
> — Pope Benedict XVI, 2009 Good Friday Address

Republicans have paid insufficient attention to the lessons that can be learned from long monarchical experience in governance.[5] In particular, no attention has been paid in the current age of democratic hegemony to the important linkages that should be formed between the office of head of state and the realm of the sacred.

Some years ago, Clifford Geertz (1983) made the pertinent observation that, in all traditional regimes, the office of head of state occupied a space that was widely believed to be sacred. In the absolutist states of the early modern era in Europe, this belief found its most forceful expression in the doctrine of the Divine Right of Kings. As long as this doctrine remained unchallenged, government attained the highest levels of legitimacy. What could be more legitimating for a regime than God's blessing?

We are not yet finished with Geertz. He goes on to assert that the sacredness of central authority persists in modern regimes: 'Sovereignty may rest now in states or even in the population of states…but the "vast universality" that inheres in it remains, whatever has become of the will of kings' (Geertz 1983:146). With the growth of secularism and the decline of monarchical institutions, this level of legitimacy is no longer available. We shall have to make do with a different,

---

5   One of Australia's leading historians, Alan Atkinson (1993:122), has convincingly shown how the monarchy long 'symbolised the moral purpose of government'. He seems completely at a loss, however, when it comes to a consideration of the ways in which this moral purpose might be recovered when the influence of the monarchy declines. The best he can come up with is a weird proposal that the Australian monarchy could be 'reconstituted', either through the British royals spending more time in Australia or through royal acquiescence in the installation of a cousin as the Australian monarch.

more contingent form of regime legitimation. While most republicans are quite happy to accept this trade-off between level and form of legitimacy, two implications should be openly recognised.

First, much of the continuing support for the monarchist cause doubtless stems from the respect of its adherents for some awe-inspiring remnants of the old sacred space. Second, republicans should appreciate that they are being asked to endorse a more contingent form of government legitimacy.

This new form of legitimation could appropriately also be described as fiducial—resting on a constantly renewed pact between the citizenry and those responsible for ensuring the integrity of our major institutions. To date, fiducial activity has been seen as being undertaken only spasmodically: at times of regime founding, such as the referendum that established the Australian Federation at the beginning of the past century. Some theorists, most notably Wolin (1996), have contended that only in such rare moments can democracy be said to be fully alive. As we shall soon see, however, the prominence accorded by Ackerman to serial referenda in his framework of constrained parliamentarianism opens up the possibility of widening such opportunities for democratic legitimation. In such a manner, the sacred space once occupied by the head of state will be replaced with a form of democratic legitimation less robust but more suited to the current age.

A proper understanding of the importance of the sacred and of the ways in which it could be revived in a modern secular democracy is essential for the achievement of a republic worth having. We cannot be confident about the trustworthiness of our major institutions without the existence of a 'sacred' core.[6] One useful understanding of the sacred conceptualises it as '[h]aving symbolic value and thus, like good music, facilitat(ing) the evolution of the group' (Lundy 2002).[7]

Just what would be the role of the State in facilitating the evolution of the national group is a hazardous task best left to authoritative collegial bodies, such as the councils of state whose creation I shall be recommending. This monograph will thus be concerned, inter alia, to suggest provisional agendas for such bodies, together with brief rationales for the inclusion of the agenda items proposed.

---

6   Keane (2009:16) pertinently observes that there was a close association between democracy and the sacred in ancient Athens.
7   Eisler (1995: 21) holds a similar conception, linking it to 'the power to give, nurture and illuminate life...'

e) Ubiquity in governance of imputation

I first became aware of the importance of imputation when I came to consider the implications for modern governance of Friedrich's magisterial work *Man and His Government* (1963)—in particular, the conception of authority around which much of his argument rested. According to Friedrich, authority is the capacity for reasoned elaboration in terms of the values, interests and beliefs shared by the authority wielder and those subject to its exercise. The politics of governance, however, require an extension of this understanding, for what is of the utmost importance is the fact that the authority wielder is not required to provide such elaboration in justification of every decision. Authority is the most effective form of power in governance precisely because its exercise is usually not questioned, which allows the public authority wielder to get on with the work of governing. The capacity for reasoned elaboration is imputed to the authority wielder by those subject to that authority.

Thus, imputation is central to my understanding of public authority and governance. As with authority, policies are the purposive constructions that are imputed by interested publics to the actions and resource commitments of those in authority. Of course, those in authority will never be backward in advancing their own purposive constructions, but what is of the highest political significance is the extent to which interested publics are prepared to accept these authoritative constructions. Sometimes they have good grounds for doubting the purposive constructions that have been advanced from on high. More commonly, interested publics will concede some validity to these constructions. Indeed, the authentication of these authoritative constructions is a central element in any responsible system of governance.

As authority is the most pervasive basis for public power, its putative nature poses a central political problem for republicanism. To have a capacity imputed to a public leader is a great benefit to that person, and it is such a benefit that it easily slides into a distaste for ever being called on to validate authority through the real demonstration of the capacity for the reasoned elaboration that has been imputed. This tendency is especially pronounced when the public leader holds a position in a state structure, for much of the affairs of state must always be transacted in a setting of confidentiality; hence, 'reasons of state'.

Thus authority all too easily morphs into authoritarianism, when the holder of a public office comes to believe that there is no longer any need for the imputed capacity to be validated. Fiducial governance must resist this tendency wherever it manifests itself, for the bedrock of such governance is genuine authority. It is therefore of the highest political significance that the authority wielder should be regularly held to account. But how regular is regular?

Clearly, the frequency and indeed the nature of the interrogation of the authority wielder will vary from one setting to another, so we could expect considerable variation among the councils of state as they establish their responsibility systems. There is much that inevitably is implicit in the exercise and testing of authority, and nowhere is this tendency stronger than in the realms of confidentiality that are always at the centre of many of the most important concerns of a head of state. The republican style of governance requires regular critical inspection of claims of confidentiality. These claims will often prove justified, but a republican public is always entitled to some form of vouching, where a trusted governance leader who has been privy to considerations of confidential matters testifies as to their integrity.

f) Constraining executives

The orthodox Australian position on the accountability of our political executives has most recently received clear expression from Rhodes and Wanna (2009:129): 'Networks not only obscure accountability but they pose a challenge to executive co-ordination, and require different management skills to bureaucracy or contracts. They open a major research agenda.'

Apparently, Rhodes and Wanna did not consider it part of their brief to go beyond the identification of research opportunities to consider some of the normative issues raised by constraining reforms aimed at making our executives more clearly accountable. For the best recent example of such an endeavour, we must turn to the British governance practitioner, Geoff Mulgan.

Although he uses terminology differently to the ways in which I am using it, Mulgan's 2006 work, *Good and Bad Power*, presents an excellent opportunity for the further opening up of many of the issues concerned with fiducial governance.

For Mulgan, the primary problem for the attainment of good governance can be stated simply: the purpose of governments is everywhere to serve the interests of their constituents. Possession of the state power needed to realise good governance is, however, so valuable a resource that the state apparatus will always attract those who wish to use it for the furtherance of their own particular interests, often to the detriment of the public interest.

In order to counteract this ever-present danger, Mulgan (2006:319) proposes the establishment of a set of 'aligned' constraints (which he terms 'devices that force governments to live up to their roles as servants'):

- contestability through election
- divisions of power
- the rule of law
- visibility, free media and free access to information.

All four of these constraints need to be properly 'aligned' if they are to enhance the trust that the citizenry has in the integrity of the institutions that govern them. In other words, this alignment is necessary for the attainment of fiducial governance. Mulgan, however, does not go far beyond identifying the necessity for such alignment; he does not identify an institutional mechanism that could take the lead in developing such a mechanism. (One infers that the responsibility for this alignment will in Mulgan's view remain the responsibility of the very interests that seek to profit from inside access to state powers. *Quis custodiet ipsos custodes?*)

One reason for Mulgan's inability to go further stems from his failure to distinguish the State from government. Once such a distinction is made, it becomes possible to distinguish the fiducial governance roles of heads of state from the executive roles of heads of governments. It is the former that is best equipped to lead in the discharge of this governance function, if only because s/he is usually better placed to secure the trust of the citizenry. The strong support of heads of government will be necessary for the establishment of a viable mechanism to work on these fiducial tasks, but the head of government must in day-to-day political life always be most sensitive to the needs of his/her party and the interests that have clustered around it.

Because Mulgan has avoided the formalism that inevitably accompanies efforts to draft proposals for constitutional reform, he has been able to explore very perceptively the interrelations that should exist between governments and their citizenry. His is therefore an outstanding contribution to what an earlier work described as 'societal constitutionalism' (Sciulli 1992). As this monograph is ultimately about constitutional reform, however, we must bite the bullet and attempt to render the subtle Mulgan argument in more formalistic terms. It is at this point that the work of the comparatist Ackerman is of the greatest use.

Constrained parliamentarianism

In the way that Ackerman has developed the framework, constrained parliamentarianism offers the prospect of maintaining a measure of coherence as we struggle to comprehend the bewildering array of institutions now becoming enmeshed in processes of governance. We can speak of no more than a prospect at this stage because the theory of constrained parliamentarianism, for all its considerable virtues, is itself still underdeveloped.[8] If we understand by 'constraint' a limit than can support as it restrains,[9] we can assert that the theory of constrained parliamentarianism needs itself to be more heavily constrained.

The great virtue of the Ackerman polyarchical framework is that it enables us to assess differing institutional arrangements through use of a good governance value base, which has three 'legitimating ideals':

> The first ideal is democracy. In one way or another, separation may serve (or hinder) the project of popular self-government. The second ideal is professional competence. Democratic laws remain purely symbolic unless courts and bureaucracies can implement them in a relatively impartial way. The third ideal is the protection and enhancement of fundamental rights. (Ackerman 2000:640)

Ackerman proceeds to discuss the principal constraints on executive power—on my reading of him, seven—that serve these ideals. The relations between the ideals and the constraints are shown in Table 1.1.

Although the bulk of his long paper is devoted to the exploration of these relationships and their implications, Ackerman also goes on to consider a long-neglected topic: how the creation of new branches of governance could enable us to overcome some of the inadequacies of existing sets of institutional arrangements.[10] As Ackerman (2000:727) puts it: 'The power of this center[11] is checked and balanced by a host of special-purpose Branches, each motivated by one or more of the three basic concerns of separationist theory.'

---

8   Like many Americans who have been unduly influenced by the reading of Montesquieu by their founding fathers, Ackerman (2000:695, n. 138, where he describes a prime minister as a head of state) is unclear about the fundamental distinction between head of state and head of government. It is for this reason that I have found it necessary to add an important further element to the Ackerman framework of constrained parliamentarianism: a viable role for the head of state.

9   This positive if contingent understanding of constraint is one that is shared by Ackerman (2005:106) himself: 'If we are lucky in our leaders, they will look upon the emergency constitution in a favorable light: rather than seeing it as an obstacle, blocking their reach for arbitrary power, they will appreciate how it enhances their legitimate authority to act decisively at times of national crisis.' The sense, if not the term itself, seems also to be present in the observation of Patapan (2000:2) that checks can sustain.

10   It is at this point that the virtues of the Ackerman approach are most readily appreciated. In many important respects, his value base strongly resembles the 'liberal democratic' base proposed by Kukathas et al. (1990). Ackerman, however, proceeds from this base to the specification of an extensive reform program, whereas Kukathas et al. ultimately have little to propose except a sceptical negativism.

11   Curiously, Ackerman (2000:727) places the Parliament at this 'centre': 'As the centerpeice of my model of constrained parliamentarism is a democratically elected house in charge of selecting a government and enacting ordinary legislation.' The centrepiece to be constrained in any parliamentarian system is not, however, the legislature, but rather the political executive: 'A cabinet is a combining committee—a *hyph*en which joins, a *buckle* which fastens, the legislative part of the state to the executive part of the state. In its origins it belongs to the one, in its functions it belongs to the other' (Bagehot 1872:71–2). All political executives are quite properly constrained. Even the traditional sovereign supremacy of the British Parliament was in practice constrained by numerous practices and conventions, and in recent years many of these have become expressed explicitly in legal instruments, some of them not readily negated by Westminster itself (to the point that one distinguished British scholar has been brought to ask whether his nation still has a constitution [King 2001]).

Table 1.1 Ackerman's values and constraints

Ideal	Democracy	Professional competency	Citizen rights
Federal structure	'[T]he (democratically elected) center may...be checked by a subordinate federal senate.' (p. 727)		
Strong upper house	'Although the [Japanese] upper House of Councillors has significant powers, it is not the constitutional equal of the lower House. Call this the "one-and-a-half house solution".' (p. 635)		
Professional public service and integrity of major institutions		'From the side of functional specialization, the center is constrained not only by an independent court system, but also by an integrity branch scrutinizing the government for corruption and similar abuses.' (p. 727)	
Independent judiciary	'Democratic laws remain purely symbolic unless courts and bureaucracies can implement them in a relatively impartial way.' (p. 640)	'We will require a constitutional court to make the principles enacted by the people ... into operational realities.' (p. 668)	
Securing human rights			'[A] constitution ought to constrain the exercise of democratic self-rule by protecting fundamental individual rights.' (p. 722)
Serial referenda	'[W]e should seek to divide [lawmaking authority] between parliament and the people—the former managing routine governmental decisions and the latter expressing its will through a carefully constructed process of serial referenda.' (p. 668)		

From Ackerman (2000).

Central to Ackerman's approach to structure, then, is his grouping together of diverse functions in branches of government. He builds on the familiar triad—legislative, executive, judicial—and goes on to identify a fourth, bureaucracy, and to recommend a further four: integrity, regulatory, democracy and distributive justice. In addition, he has more recently recommended the establishment of a decency commission (Ackerman 2005:112 ff.).

If we were to agree that the recognition of a new branch of government is not something that should be advanced lightly, we might well respect Addison's warning that there should not be more than four (see Preface, fn 1). If we decided to restrict ourselves to one further branch, which should it be? For those with a particular commitment to fiducial governance, the claims of a branch concerned primarily with institutional integrity are of the highest significance.

Each of the universally recognised three branches is headed by a collegial body (cabinet, supreme court, legislative chamber), is led by an identifiable officer (head of government, chief justice, speaker) and has a process (as contrasted with a goal) orientation. Any new branch should exhibit the same characteristics. But what should it be called?

I propose to appropriate a term recently introduced by Keane (2009): 'monitory.' This serves my purposes better than the Ackerman term that has attracted a measure of support in Australia—'integrity'—because it refers to a process, whereas the latter term refers to a goal.[12]

h) A monitory branch

In his recent important book, Keane (2009) has drawn our attention to the systemic significance of the sets of monitory institutions (for example, regulatory and anti-corruption commissions, parliamentary committees, auditors and ombudsmen, and so on) that have appeared in most jurisdictions in recent decades. As he points out, since 1945 modern democracies have witnessed the birth of nearly 100 new types of power-scrutinising institutions (Keane 2009:690).[13] So significant have these become, in Keane's view, that he has advanced the claim—one that has been widely noted—that a new form of regime now exists: monitory democracy. The next step—which Keane has

---

12 I explore this issue more fully in a paper to the 2010 Public Policy Network Conference: 'Monitory democracy—or a monitory branch of a democratic regime?'.
13 Coming from another direction—public sector employment—Nelson (2008:56 ff.) has recently come to a conclusion that supports the argument of Keane, for she claims that the activities of national governments have in recent years been becoming increasingly monitory.

not yet taken—is to explore the ways in which republicanism could further the purposes of monitory democracy. And in this enterprise, the work of Braithwaite (1998, and especially 2008) is relevant.

Indeed, it is striking that in his work on monitory democracy, Keane (2009) does not pay attention to the ways in which Braithwaite (2008) had earlier treated much the same phenomenon from the different perspective of 'regulatory capitalism'. Both examine the ways in which republican measures of explicitness have proliferated in recent years, with the former focusing on government institutions and the latter on those associated with governance. Yet neither one is capable of moving on to examine the ways in which these measures might be properly coordinated, as they should be in any responsible regime, for neither has explored the ways in which head-of-state offices might be developed in ways that promote the democratic ideal of polyarchy (which I discuss more fully below).

Given the ubiquity of imputation, republican theorising must inevitably be trailing behind the adoption of measures that might forward the republican cause. For example, Australian monarchists are fond of claiming that we already have a 'crowned republic', because we possess many regulatory and monitory institutions. They do not go on, however, to assess the quality of the republican regime that has been gradually emerging, for such an exploration would require attention to possible republican changes to our head-of-state offices.

In the following striking passage from Braithwaite (2008:85), such an exploration is begun:

> [A] republican who values freedom as non-domination (Braithwaite 1997; Pettit 1997) cannot want a separation of powers where each branch of governance is left alone to misuse power without too much interference within its own sphere from the other branches of government. Rather, for the complex world of regulatory capitalism, republican freedom requires many separations of private and public powers, not just three branches of state governance…No single branch of governance is allowed to dominate because, as it seeks to dominate another branch, that branch's interdependence with third and fourth branches will protect its semi-autonomy.

In this passage, Braithwaite shows clearly the close connections between the central republican goal of freedom as non-domination and the integrity of regulatory and monitory institutions. He does not, however, take the next republican step, which is to investigate the ways in which heads of state might effect polyarchical coordination—that is, the shaping of mutual influences towards purposefulness that falls well short of attempted domination. There are two dimensions to the achievement of such coordination. First, as Braithwaite recognises, recognition of the need for a fresh look at the ways powers are separated in existing machineries of governance—and here the work of Ackerman is of the highest importance. Second, we face the need for a fresh look at possible new head-of-state roles. Let us take these two dimensions in turn.

The limitations of the language we use often have a significant effect on the form and content of political argumentation. For example, we currently lack a term in common use to describe the regime most conducive to democratic government. A generation ago, the leading modern student of democracy, Dahl (1971), introduced the term 'polyarchy' to fill this gap, but the term has never enjoyed common usage. It deserves to, for reasons I shall now outline.

Because of its pluralist connotations, polyarchy seems appropriate to the purpose of describing a regime well suited to the support of democratic government. As Dahl (1971:8) put it, 'polyarchies are regimes that have been substantially popularized and liberalized, that is, highly inclusive and extensively open to public contestation'. The constraints that legitimately bind and support democratic governments derive from a polyarchical culture. The 'fit' between regime and form of government is, however, as Dahl himself reminds us, always imperfect. So the tasks of republican governance are never finished and heads of states should be centrally involved in tackling these tasks.

For the study of comparative politics, I suggest three levels of analysis[14] of governance, each with its own characteristic suffix

- *-archy* denotes a governance regime, in which internal and external relations are integrated; one whose jurisdictional boundaries are coterminous with those of the modern nation-state ('mon-', 'poly-', 'olig-', 'an-')
- *-cracy*[15] denotes the ways in which a government handles the 'external' relations between the rulers and the ruled ('demo-', 'auto-', 'aristo-', 'cosmo-'[16])

---

14 We should here note the appropriation by economics of another suffix, which would otherwise have been of obvious promise for political purposes: '-poly', as in 'mono-' and 'oligo-'.

15 Terms that possess a '-cracy' suffix—'demo-', 'auto-', 'aristo-'—all relate to the style and composition of governments. If their meaning is stretched so as to attempt to cover the regime supporting a particular form of government, as in much ideological rhetoric about democratisation, many assumptions about key relationships—such as those between the form of government and the structure of interests in the civil society and culture—are made and then have to be covered up. The outcome, as Little (2008) has recently argued, has been the promulgation of 'democratic piety'.

16 This is a term coined a few years ago by Keane (2003:98), who defined it as follows: 'A conglomeration of interlocking and overlapping sub-state, state and suprastate institutions and multi-dimensional processes that interact, and have political and social effects, on a global scale.' While there are some similarities between this concept and Keane's later 'monitory democracy', two important differences should be noted. Most obviously, the scope of the two differs, with one being focused on the globe and the other on the nation-state. Less immediately obvious, perhaps, is the relative importance of government in the two constructs, for it is much more influential at the level of the nation-state than at the global.

- *-ism* denotes 'internal' relations between the branches of governance, especially between the Executive and the legislature ('presidential-', 'semi-presidential-', 'parliamentar-').[17]

Before proceeding any further, a cautionary note should be struck. Many of the terms that are central to the study of comparative politics—such as 'regime', 'government' and 'governance' itself—are not susceptible to this treatment. The use of the schema is therefore limited.

Nevertheless, the suffix schema can with benefit be compared with the earlier 'levels' schema proposed by Kiser and Ostrom (1982). Table 1.2 compares the two schemas.

Table 1.2 Two schemas focusing on 'levels' compared

Kiser and Ostrom analytical level	'Suffix' level	Comparative comment
Operational	-ism	The central role at this level is an 'internal' one and relates to the most operationally oriented of the branches of government—the Executive—in all the machinery of government '-isms' mentioned above.
Collective	-cracy	This is the level at which the particular nature of public authority characteristic of a regime is most clearly articulated. It is thus primarily 'external' to government.
Constitutional	-archy	In both schemas, this is the level at which the most entrenched rules are to be found. Usually, these are embedded in a particular political culture. It is at this level that fundamental balances between the internal and external dimensions are struck.

In the discussion that follows, I shall, in the next section, which is concerned with the dimensions of constrained parliamentarianism, follow this 'top-down' order, so as to deal first with those elements that relate most strongly to the '-archy' level, then with those that bear most strongly on the '-cracy' level, and finally those concerned with the '-isms'. Having done this, I shall move on to a consideration of an element largely ignored by Ackerman but one that is central to my reform program: viable head-of-state roles. So important is this dimension that I devote the whole of Section 3 to a discussion of its role and character.

Finally, in the concluding Section 4, I revisit the dimensions of constrained parliamentarianism, but, because of the transformation that could be accomplished by the new head-of-state dimension, in reverse, 'bottom-up'

---

17 Of course, there are several other '-isms' that should here be noted, although they refer primarily to ideologies and thus are not directly relevant to the concerns of the current paper: 'totalitarian-', 'fasc-', 'naz-', 'commun-', 'social-'. The '-isms' with which this monograph is concerned are those that have to do with machinery of government issues.

order. I end with an account of what remains, suitably constrained, the centre of any framework of good governance: republican parliamentary democracy. In this way, I can most conveniently set the context for a constructively critical if brief assessment of the concept of monitory democracy.

i) Republican parliamentary governance: a lesson from Australia's Indigenous peoples

It will be amply apparent by now that I favour an indirect approach to the attainment of republican governance. Indeed, one of my expert readers questioned whether I was really committed to the republican cause at all!

My response is a simple one: the minimalist approach favoured by the mainstream of the republican movement (led by the ARM but including some of our major parties as well) has been, and will continue to be, seriously flawed. Some recent thinking among members of our Indigenous community indicates a way in which some of these flaws may be remedied.

When compared with other nations with substantial indigenous populations, Australia has to date refused to grant its own Indigenous peoples reserved representation. This gap could, however, certainly be filled in the constitution of each of the proposed councils of state. The recent report *Our Future in Our Hands: Creating a sustainable national representative body for Aboriginal and Torres Strait Islander peoples* (Australian Human Rights Commission 2009b) provides sound guidance—not only on the question of how Indigenous representatives might best be located in the proposed new bodies, but on the broader questions concerned with the selection of the most appropriate processes that should be developed in the establishment of the councils of state themselves.

Unsurprisingly, in the light of the fluctuating fortunes of and ultimate frustrations with the Aboriginal and Torres Strait Islander Commission (ATSIC, which was abolished with bipartisan agreement in 2005), the leaders of the Australian Indigenous community have had to do some original thinking when it came to the development of proposals that entailed the insertion of new bodies into already crowded machinery of government domains. They therefore proposed the fashioning of three 'chambers' to stand between the Indigenous electorate, on the one hand, and a national representative body, to be called the National Congress of Australia's First Peoples, on the other.

This 'three-chamber' strategy could easily be adapted to further the cause of fiducial governance[18]

---

18   As it will be up to each council of state to determine how it might shape its internal structure in the light of developments in other relevant jurisdictions, I have identified only the most obvious starting institutions for each chamber.

- chamber 1: national peak bodies (representatives from the three established branches of government[19]; from the National Congress of Australia's First Peoples)
- chamber 2: sectoral peak bodies (representatives from the Council of Australian Governments; from other councils of state)
- chamber 3: local community and individual representatives[20] (representatives from the interests represented in the Australian Collaboration and from those representing interests not specifically covered by the Collaboration (for example, women, the aged, the disabled).

---

19 Although it would be optimal for fiducial governance if each judicial branch were accorded full membership in its Council of State, it has to be acknowledged that, as they stand, the constitutions of many Australian jurisdictions would not permit this. Accordingly, 'weaker' forms of representation (of the kind identified in Chapter 4) would be the best hoped for, until the climate of consitutional reform improved.

20 The Australian Collaboration was created in 2000, with the following membership: Australian Council of Social Service; Australian Conservation Foundation; Australian Consumers Association; Australian Council for International Development; Federation of Ethnic Communities' Councils of Australia; National Council of Churches in Australia; Trust for Young Australians; Representative of indigenous population (now the National Congress of Australia's First Peoples).

2. The current Australian regime

a) Strengths and weaknesses of the current regime

The most recent comprehensive assessment of the current Australian regime, *Australia: The state of democracy*, lists no fewer than 50 strengths and 58 weaknesses, although it does not go on to recommend explicit reform strategies for improvement (Sawer et al. 2009). It does, however, supply us with a useful checklist for setting a context for the discussion of six of our eight sections below.[1]

Perusal of the more than 100 items of assessment that follow shows that *Australia: The state of democracy* follows a fairly standard left-liberal line, being particularly concerned with the effects of anti-terrorism laws and with the inequitable treatments still meted out to Indigenous Australians and many asylum-seekers. This inclination should be constantly borne in mind as we move through the categories of the constrained parliamentarianism framework. (As the purpose of *Australia: The state of democracy* differs from that of this monograph, some of the item 'placements' will be fairly rough and ready; despite this, they perform the service required of them, for they provide a good context for evaluation.)

b) Parliamentary democracy

Table 2.1 Parliamentary democracy

Context set by Sawer et al. (2009:24, 126, 146, 171, 230, 245, 276, 293)

Strengths	Weaknesses
An immigration policy oriented towards permanent residence and the granting of citizenship Many of the social rights generally associated with citizenship available to permanent residents	No national representative body to speak for Indigenous Australians Dual citizens precluded from membership of the Australian Parliament

---

1 Surprisingly, this report concerns itself only in passing with one of the major categories suggested by Ackerman: a strong upper house of the Commonwealth Parliament. Unsurprisingly, it, like Ackerman, ignores the possible reform roles of heads of state.

Access and equity policies in all jurisdictions to address the needs of those from culturally and linguistically diverse backgrounds	Increased stress on assimilation to 'national values'
Tradition of non-partisan electoral administration	Elections sometimes won with minority of votes
Compulsory voting ensuring high turnout	A 'shrinking' electoral roll
Some element of proportional representation in most jurisdictions	Parliamentary under-representation of women, immigrants and Indigenous Australians
Elections usually produce decisive results with clear winners and losers	Public funding has supplemented rather than replaced private funding
Attempts to improve internal party democracy	Inadequate disclosure regime for political donations
Despite globalisation, government retains control over key areas of policy	Low party membership
Systematic scrutiny of government expenditure	Executive dominance of parliament
Strong bicameralism in most jurisdictions	Limited parliamentary role in authorising public expenditure
Independent, publicly funded national broadcasters	Relatively weak freedom-of-information culture and laws
Generally free news media	Lack of accountability of ministerial advisers
Greater uniformity in defamation laws	Lack of transparency in government appointments to boards
Increased self-scrutiny by media industry	High concentration of media ownership
High level of participation in voluntary associations	Increased political and financial pressures on public broadcasting
Presence of women in public office increasing	Tighter restrictions on reporting due to anti-terrorism laws
New approaches to public consultation	Prospect of prison for journalists who protect sources
Accessibility of elected representatives	Weak political representation of new immigrant groups
High level of satisfaction with government services	Muting of non-governmental organisation advocacy through conditions attached to public funding
Local government acts now require community consultation	Lack of independent regulator for charities
Increased attention to integrity systems	Declining levels of trust in government
Recognition of local government in most state constitutions	Unmet need for many services
History of support for international human rights initiatives	Slow uptake of deliberative processes
Support for democratic capacity building in the region	Lack of recognition of local government in the Australian Constitution
Proactive in providing market access for poorer countries	Continued existence of property votes in most jurisdictions
Parliamentary oversight of treaty making	Financial weakness of local government
	'Efficiency' reforms, including amalgamations, at expense of democracy
	Variable relationship with the United Nations over human rights
	Little community input into objectives for treaty negotiation
	Skewing of foreign aid program to fit strategic objectives
	Failure to meet UN target for volume of overseas aid

The exhaustive Sawer checklist in Table 2.1—with its 27 'strengths' and 32 'weaknesses'—enables us to make a balanced judgment on the current condition of Australian parliamentary democracy. The most prominent theme that emerges from a reading of these lists is the way in which the formal provisions of a constitution that is now more than a century old are still so heavily influential. And it has been in those areas that are more difficult to shape through formal constitutional provision that weaknesses have become most apparent. So, if we are to move towards fiducial governance, we need to compensate for one major shift that has occurred during the nation's existence, although it has been ignored by Sawer—the weakening of the influence of the Crown—an influence that was all too prominent when the constitution was being drafted. And as we move to specify the reforms needed to compensate for this weakening, we can learn some important lessons from one set of citizens who were extremely poorly recognised in that same drafting process of the 1890s: Indigenous Australians.

As we have already noted above (in Section 1k), the recent report *Our Future in Our Hands* provides sound guidance not only on the question of how Indigenous representatives might best be located in the proposed new bodies, but on the broader questions concerned with the selection of the most appropriate processes that should be established in the development of the councils of state themselves.

c) Federal structure[2]

Table 2.2 Federal structure

Context set by Sawer et al. (2009:310)

Strengths	Weaknesses
Scope for policy innovation and experimentation More opportunities for political participation Potential for regional responsiveness and diversity Fiscal equalisation to ensure services of equal standard	Limited scope in intergovernmental decision making for parliamentary deliberation or community consultation Lack of transparency in intergovernmental decision making Accountability issues arising from blame-shifting and confusion

The most recent review of the condition of Australian federalism (Fenna 2009:155) concluded that there was little compelling reason to support the continuation of the system, for there 'has been the apparent absence of any

---

2   It had been my expectation that a recent monograph in this series (Brown and Bellamy 2007) would provide much that could be valuable for this project. Brown is after all a first–class scholar, and one who had played a leading role in the earlier NISA project (Griffith University 2005) that had paid considerable attention to the importance of institutional integrity for governance regimes in Australia. I was, however, to be disappointed, for Brown ignored the NISA report in the later work.

sociological basis for divided jurisdiction in this country'. It could be, however, that there are other reasons—such as improvement in the quality of governance through a regime of serial referenda—that could still be persuasive. The best of the students of modern Australian federalism, Brian Galligan, has attempted to show how strong popular involvement has imparted republican legitimacy to the system.

Although the most important recent work on Australian federalism has thus been Galligan's *A Federal Republic* (1995), this work would have been even better if it had dealt more fully with head-of-state roles. Galligan searchingly uncovered and criticised a number of the premises that had long dominated thinking about the Australian constitutional system. His great accomplishment is to demonstrate that all the various proponents of responsible government have paid insufficient attention to the considerable constraints that have been placed on all our governments and their constituent branches by our federal constitutional framework. These constraints are, in Galligan's (1995:14) view, appropriate and legitimate, because federation entailed a 'transformative act of the Australian people'. In this respect, he is aligning himself with one of the two traditions that have dominated Australia's 'dual constitutional culture': the federal (which Galligan favours) and parliamentary responsible government (Galligan 1995:50).

Galligan's (1995:14) central proposition is that Australia already possesses a republic, 'because the constitutions, for both the Commonwealth and the States, are the instruments of the Australian people who have supreme authority'. The people are claimed to have exercised this authority because they democratically approved the constitution at the end of the nineteenth century and since then have had to approve in referenda any further formal changes. This regime is a 'crowned republic' because the Australian people considered the monarchy appropriate to the needs of the federating nation (Galligan 1995:18).

There are, however, serious problems with this argument. Galligan's rather too-ready acceptance of the monarchist slogan that Australia is already a crowned republic passes over the very considerable tensions that exist between the monarchical and republican styles of governance.

The fact that our forebears considered the Crown to be a central feature of the legitimation of the new constitution has led to the continuation to the present day of much of the 'good chaps' culture of governance, especially but not only in gubernatorial offices. And sometimes the 'good chaps' have not been up to the task of policy development in a federal system. As Sawer and her colleagues (2009:295) have recently observed, 'The system creates subnational "veto points" that can obstruct policy which a national government has been elected to enact and hence frustrates "the will of the people".'

This leads us to a second problem and that is whether the contemporary citizenry will be satisfied that it has participated sufficiently in the shaping of our constitutional framework for it to be accorded full democratic legitimacy.

Unlike Galligan, who has been quite content to contend that the necessary constitutional legitimation was achieved in Australia in the one founding moment more than a century ago,[3] Ackerman (2007:1800) explicitly considers the implications of long lapses in time: 'It is one thing for South Africans or Germans to follow a constitution handed down a decade, or a half-century, ago; quite another for Americans to cling to an antique text that fails to mark any of the nation's recent achievements.'

Galligan is thus insufficiently critical in his assessment of the Australian constitutional arrangements. He is so intent on demonstrating that much of the needed reforms of our governance can be achieved through 'subconstitutional institutions' (Galligan 1995:37) that he is insufficiently sensitive to some of the tensions that underlie our system.

How well does the Australian regime handle these tensions, which are inescapable in any republic? In other words, how good is our republic? This is a question Galligan does not directly address. Instead, he contents himself with several iterations of a populist point: that the people usually have more sense than the 'expert' elites who frequently distrust them. Because the Turnbull report was based on 'an interpretive tradition of arid legalism' (Galligan 1995:25), it lacked the faith in the good judgment of the Australian people that ultimately led Galligan (1999) to support direct election of the head of state.

It is, however, surely possible to develop the Galligan argument further. He (1995:135) has himself noted the 'patchwork of human rights measures' that has emerged in recent years. He has also stressed the need for a strengthening of the consensual elements in our public life (Galligan 1995:132, 213). These two themes have subsequently been linked in the 2005 NISA report, which called for recognition of a separate governance review council. Neither Galligan nor NISA has, however, given consideration to the ways in which those playing roles in head-of-state offices might be able to take the lead in the development of such bodies, which could substantially strengthen the consensual dimensions of public life.

---

3   It should be acknowledged, however, that even long-distant public affirmations could be of fiducial significance. As Zines (2008:557) puts it: 'The concept of sovereignty of the people, therefore, must be regarded as either purely symbolic or theoretical. Seen as a symbol it might be regarded as similar to the symbol of the Crown, uniting the various organs and elements of the organisation of government under one concept.'

d) Strong upper house

Bicameralism does not sit easily with Westminster regimes. As the Abbe Sieyes observed long ago, if the governing party controls the upper house, much of what that house does is superfluous. If, on the other hand, the government of the day does not control the upper house, much of what it does will be obstructive (Uhr 2008:13).[4] Upper houses retain their attractiveness, however, for the more consensually minded democrats, for in most jurisdictions they have shown greater readiness than their lower house colleagues to become involved in policy development through committee activity (Halligan et al. 2007).

In modern democratic times, the balance of power has shifted towards lower houses in most bicameral regimes. In the Australian states, for example, most upper houses have lost much of their blocking powers. Contemporary theorising has also followed this trend; thus Ackerman's framework of constrained parliamentarianism envisages an upper house with only 'half' powers.

Although Ackerman (2000:671 ff.) gives some consideration to federalism as one of the constraints in his framework, he does so in a curiously limited way. His discussion of federalism is devoted almost totally to the ways in which it can shape upper houses at the national level. And in his advocacy of German-style 'half-house' upper houses, he gives insufficient attention to the optimal balance that should be struck between the powers of an upper house, on the one hand, and its effectiveness, on the other. The Australian experience suggests that a 'half-house' upper house might not be powerful enough to be properly effective and that greater powers might therefore be desirable, even though these powers might very occasionally be misused. In addition, Ackerman's focus on the relation between federalism and his preferred 'one and a half' legislature raises a serious problem that he does not consider. Upper houses in federal systems are more likely to be in serious political conflict with their lower houses than are upper houses in unitary systems (Tsebelis and Money 1997:212).

There have been strong voices expressing a view contrary to that of Ackerman— that accountability should weigh more heavily than democracy. Consider, for example, some of the arguments recently advanced in the revealingly entitled volume *Restraining Elective Dictatorship: The upper house solution*.

In the opening chapter of the volume, the editors make the important point that 'an institution with its own democratic credentials constitutes a far more substantial accountability hurdle than any creation of ordinary statute law'

---

4 A recent innovation in Singapore has shown how the review function so often associated with upper houses might in a unicameral regime be discharged by another institution—in the case of Singapore, none other than a directly elected presidency (Tan 1997)!

(Prasser et al. 2008:6). They do not, however, go beyond the Parliament in their search for appropriate democratic mechanisms for holding the Executive to account. Like all the contributors that follow them, they do not directly address the problem caused by rigid party discipline. Instead, they seem to assume that the benefits of having an upper house that lacks a government majority will always outweigh the costs.

e) Professional public service

Table 2.3 Professional public service

Context set by Sawer et al. (2009:183)

Strengths	Weaknesses
The police and the military effectively under civilian control All police services subject to institutionalised civilian oversight Increased intergovernmental cooperation in efforts against organised crime	Lack of accountability in outsourced quasi-policing activities Inadequate resourcing of intelligence services watchdog Lack of diversity in police and armed services and continuing harassment issues

There is sufficient testimony to the extent of politicisation of our public services to justify a searching examination by a council of state. No-one alive is better placed than former senior minister and governor-general Bill Hayden to offer a judgment here, and he (2008:xii–xiii) considers the process of politicisation to be 'well advanced in the Commonwealth'.

When they came to consider the ways in which the integrity of the public services could best be secured in an age of 'political management', Halligan and Power unsurprisingly commented favourably on a then recent proposal from the Review of Public Service Management in Victoria (which Power had chaired):

> The Executive Branch would commit itself to the realization of values of equity and efficiency, in their several meanings...
>
> [The review] concluded that the principles of merit and equity [required the establishment of] a new statutory body with a focused mission—a Commission of Merit and Equity. (Halligan and Power 1992:252)

A decade and a half later, the just retired Australian Public Service Commissioner, Andrew Podger (2007), presented a powerful argument that strongly indicated that the Hayden view was correct—that power had become too heavily concentrated in the hands of the prime minister and the head of his department. It was, Podger suggested, time for administrative values to be strengthened and the Halligan/Power work had suggested a most effective way for this to be done: through the establishment of a new collegial body such as the Commission for Merit and Equity that had been recommended by the Victorian review.

How this commission would best be formed, and how it would relate to other, similar corporate bodies that have recently been recommended, such the NISA Governance Review Councils, would in each jurisdiction be matters best left to the pragmatic judgments of the collegial body that would head up a proposed monitory branch: a council of state.

f) Independent judiciary

Table 2.4 Independent judiciary

Context set by Sawer et al. (2009:44)

Strengths	Weaknesses
Independence of the judiciary Legal assistance programs to enable wider access to justice Availability of judicial review of administrative decisions	Restrictive funding guidelines for legal aid Disproportionate rates of incarceration for Indigenous Australians Inadequate protection for whistleblowers Limited access of asylum-seekers to rule of law

In the words of a former Chief Justice of the High Court, the court has 'an uneasy and ill-defined relationship with the other arms of government' (Mason in Patapan 2000:viii). The principal reason for this unsatisfactory state of affairs has been the court's clear recognition in recent years of the political dimension of much of its work. By discarding the 'apolitical' mask, the court has of course laid itself open to the claims of the underprivileged, as the Sawer et al. list of 'weaknesses' in Table 2.4 shows.

The now largely discarded 'apolitical' view was put by former High Court Chief Justice Barwick: 'the United States Supreme Court was inevitably drawn into political issues because it was required to interpret that country's Bill of Rights. Australia had no Bill of Rights, so the Australian High Court had no political questions to decide, went Barwick's extraordinary argument' (Kercher 1995:181). The discarding of one orthodoxy has, however, not yet been followed by a coherent statement of the nature and boundaries of the form of politics with which the judiciary is now grappling. In the absence of such an understanding, we find that some attorneys-general are now refusing to play the traditional roles of defenders of the judiciary when they face political attack. A council of state along the lines I am suggesting would be well placed to produce the needed coherent statement.

g) Securing human rights

Table 2.5 Securing human rights

Context set by Sawer et al. (2009:72, 98)

Strengths	Weaknesses
Generally unrestricted freedom of movement, expression, association and assembly	No national charter of rights
	Curtailment of rights by anti-terror laws
	High levels of domestic violence
No officially condoned violence or use of death penalty	Inadequate protection of human rights of asylum-seekers
Existence of a national human rights institution	Less secure employment with growth of workforce casualisation
Anti-discrimination legislation in all jurisdictions	High Indigenous and youth unemployment
	Lack of universal statutory paid maternity leave
Generally wide access to employment and social security	Persistent gender pay gap
Adequate food, shelter and clean water available to most Australians	Seventeen-year life expectancy gap between Indigenous and non-Indigenous Australians
Widespread availability of health services	
Compulsory and free school education	Growing problems of homelessness and housing affordability
Generally effective corporate governance regime	Laws restricting trade union activities

In an address to the National Press Club immediately after the release of the report of a National Human Rights Consultation Committee, Frank Brennan took the unusual step of distancing himself from one of the key recommendations of the committee that he had just been chairing. He was reported as having expressed doubts about giving the High Court power to issue declarations of incompatibility over legislation, saying this 'might not be workable'. The public is entitled to ask just what has been going on.

It would seem that the *National Human Rights Consultation Report* (Australian Human Rights Commission 2009a) has been fatally flawed by the assumption that has been questioned above: that there should only ever be three branches of governance. At no point does it question the orthodox division of government functions into just three categories: legislative, executive and judicial. As a result, it wrestles continually, but ultimately unsuccessfully, with the attainment of one of its key objectives: to respect the 'sovereignty' of parliament. This objective cannot be reconciled with the 'dialogue' approach favoured by the committee—for one very good reason. The *Australian Constitution* requires the High Court to confine its activities to judicial matters, yet any attempt to 'judicialise' a charter of human rights inevitably leads to a challenge to the sovereignty of parliament. The High Court can concern itself with any matter when there are two parties in dispute, and in human rights cases one of these parties inevitably has to be a government minister, who is also a Member of Parliament.

So why did the committee favour the 'dialogue' model, especially when it agreed that there had been precious little dialogue in the neo-Westminster regimes—in Britain, Canada, New Zealand, the Australian Capital Territory and Victoria—where it had been introduced? And why did it not give consideration to other ways in which dialogue between the leaders of the branches of government could be encouraged? The answers to both of these questions can be gained if the assumption that there can be only three branches of government is questioned. The committee favoured the dialogue model because it was the one that came closest to respecting the sovereignty of parliament; whenever the courts found that an act was incompatible with the provisions of the *Human Rights Charter*, it would not rule the new act *ultra vires*, but would simply refer the offending act back to a minister for attention. This was close, but not quite close enough. If a fourth 'monitory' branch of governance—headed up by a council of state on which the leaders of the three recognised branches were seated—were to be established, an appropriate forum for inter-branch dialogue would be available. Importantly, any judges seated on this body could discharge their functions without thereby compromising their roles on judicial matters (see Note 4 in Section 4 for Zines [2008] on judges appointed as *personae designatae*). And if heads of state were to be involved in the work of these councils of state, another important assumption—that the head of state could be safely ignored—would be exposed.[5]

h) Integrity of major institutions

Table 2.6 Integrity of major institutions

Context set by Sawer et al. (2009:205)

Strengths	Weaknesses
Corruption low on international scale Recognition by three states of the need for generalist anti-corruption commissions Public inquiry into bribery of Iraqi officials over wheat exports	No generalist anti-corruption commission at the federal level, nor in Victoria, South Australia or Tasmania Slowness to implement Bribery Convention Widespread use of government advertising for electoral purposes Lack of uniform regulation of post-separation employment of ministers Lack of uniform regulation of lobbyists

The serious 'weaknesses' in Table 2.6 have arisen because understandings of the three key elements in my argument—trust, institutional integrity and governance—have been dealt with in separate disciplinary contexts. The gap that I propose to fill with the concept of fiducial governance has come about

---

5   It is extraordinary that the Human Rights Commission report, like the NISA report before it, completely ignores the office of head of state.

because the phenomena concerned have 'fallen through the cracks'. Not one of the best recent treatments—of trust (Braithwaite 1998; Tilly 2005) and of institutional integrity (the NISA project [Griffith University 2005] and Head et al. 2008)—has satisfactorily come to grips with the political issues that inevitably surround major machinery of government design challenges. Let us consider these cases in turn.

Braithwaite (1998:370) provides a frustrating conclusion to what is otherwise an enlightening essay: 'Private and public sector ombudsmen and auditors, independent arbitrators and judiciaries, professional societies, a free press, and international institutions can all be important to nuanced institutionalization of distrust.'

But just how might this importance manifest itself? Braithwaite does not provide a clear answer to this question. In part because he does not even consider the Braithwaite essay, Tilly has even less to say about such institutional matters.

The starting point for any discussion under this heading must be the important NISA report, which has called for each Australian jurisdiction to create a 'non-partisan' governance review council to coordinate the activities of the several bodies now concerned with issues of institutional integrity. It has also stressed the need for these councils to gain 'institutional champions' (Griffith University Institute for Ethics, Governance and Law and Transparency International 2005:61); and it is hard to see how political leaders could not be prominent among these champions. NISA does not, however, show how these champions—some of whom are necessarily party leaders—could properly relate to the new councils. Indeed, the NISA report pays no attention to possible ways in which those playing head-of-state roles could become involved—an omission that would have been inconceivable in a report written a single generation ago, when 'the Crown' still loomed large in the protection of the integrity of our major institutions.[6]

The NISA (2005:68) report does amply justify its major conclusion that 'the Commonwealth should take the opportunity of a new institutional reform to inject a significant amount into its core institutional capacity' to assure integrity. Accordingly, its first two recommendations are that the Commonwealth should establish an integrity and anti-corruption commission and a governance review council, with memberships for the most part made up of the leaders of those institutions the report had earlier identified as 'core': ombudsman, auditors-

---

6   This is another assumption—that the head of state no longer has any relevance to the fostering of institutional integrity—that is hampering reform. Possibly because republicans are nervous about strengthening a head-of-state role that has traditionally been associated with the monarchy, they have ignored the possibility that a republican leader could play a significant role in integrity assurance. I have made this point in communications with the NISA secretariat and with academics associated with the NISA project, but have received no response.

general, and so on. Are these, however, sufficiently 'heavy' to provide the needed leadership, given that the report bemoans the 'lack of effective institutional champions' (p. 61) and raises the crucial question: 'Do senior political and business officeholders possess...the will to provide genuine leadership in integrity matters' (p. 62). This is *the* crucial question, for, as the report goes on to argue,

> for...the most fundamental dimension of the integrity system to work, there must also be mechanisms to ensure that appropriate parliamentary and executive standards are set and maintained, and that alleged integrity breaches can be investigated and publicly reported upon, even when it might be in the perceived self- interest of all political parties to let the truth languish. (Griffith University Institute for Ethics, Governance and Law and Transparency International 2005:85)

The report has, however, earlier stated that it 'did not reach definitive conclusions on how integrity system capacity should be developed in relation to political parties' (p. 77). It is not surprising, then, that the report considered overall progress at the Commonwealth level had been unacceptably slow and halting. It would seem that the politics of constitutional reform needs further consideration. Where might genuine political champions be found at the Commonwealth level?

The obvious place to start a search for such champions is the list of institutions provided by the report's 'mapping' exercise. And here we encounter a most surprising omission, for again there is no acknowledgment of the integrity role that is being played, or could be played, by the head of state. Inevitably, then, there is no consideration of the ways in which integrity assurance could be strengthened by the move to a republic (although there is a passing reference to Braithwaite's 'republican conception of guardianship'; p. 16). Both former Governor-General Paul Hasluck, who introduced important innovations in this area, and former Victorian Governor Richard McGarvie, who emerged a few years ago as the latest champion of the Hasluck approach, are ignored.

This lacuna is in itself testimony to the desiccated state in which the Australian monarchy now finds itself; even a single generation ago, it is inconceivable that a wide-ranging review of public integrity would have dared to omit any reference to the significance of 'the Crown'.

What is needed is a high-level collegial body with a membership similar to that of the Irish Council of State (which is discussed briefly below). The early recommendations of the NISA report could easily be reconciled with such an initiative. For example, the council of state could be requested to consider adapting the proposed integrity and anti-corruption commission so that it could serve as the council's secretariat. And the proposed governance review council could be constituted as a committee of the council of state.

The NISA project at least touched on the ways in which these several activities might be coordinated, with its recommendation that each Australian jurisdiction should establish a governance review council to discharge that purpose, but it failed to go on to examine the political issues raised by such a major restructuring of the machinery of government.

i) Serial referenda

The *Australian Constitution* has proven extremely difficult to change, with only eight proposals (of 44) being approved in referenda during more than a century. And it is now more than a decade since any referendum was put to the people. Australia is thus far away from Ackerman's preferred state—where the citizenry would regularly be accorded the opportunity to vote on major issues.

Few commentators have considered the possibility that it has been the party system that has been responsible for many of the negative votes. While it has been widely recognised that bipartisan agreement has been a necessary prerequisite for success, few have pondered the implications of the observation of one recent prime minister (John Howard) that often even the securing of such agreement might be counterproductive, in that the citizenry might have well-founded suspicions that anything that the major parties agreed on might well serve their shared interests, which might well not be the public interest.

Clearly, any reforms that improved the fiducial standing of the party system could improve the chances of referendum success, as would regular referendum experience for the citizenry. More generally, I shall be arguing below that much valuable work can be accomplished by the several councils of state and their committees before they embark on the tasks of securing popular approval through serial referenda.

j) Viable role for the head of state[7]

In his persuasive analysis of the governor's role in Australia, former Victorian Governor Richard McGarvie (1999) placed great stress on the constitutional

---

7   Throughout this monograph, I have not sought to differentiate the gubernatorial roles in the Commonwealth and state/territory jurisdictions, although I recognise that the specifics of these roles will require the careful attention of each council of state.

counselling function. Because governors are in effect chosen by prime ministers and premiers, they are sufficiently trusted to be accepted as providers of continuing confidential counsel to ministers requiring royal assent to their respective pieces of legislation. McGarvie drew two important lessons from his analysis: the governor-general has to be trusted by the government of the day and therefore should continue to be selected by it; and the governor-general should continue to have substantial formal executive powers, so that ministers have to come to him or her with requests for formal assent. Ex-ministers to whom I have spoken have confirmed the value to them of this counsel.

In addition, McGarvie subtly explores the relationship between Australian heads of government and their governors. He demonstrates that this relationship—one of increasing importance in securing stability of governance throughout our nation's first century—is based solidly on conventions backed by sanctions. The chief minister and his/her governor are locked together in a structure of mutual deterrence. Each may, at considerable cost, secure the dismissal of the other but, knowing this, each of them customarily desists. This is a most important 'buffer' protecting both the chief minister and the pair sharing the responsibilities of the head of state.

More recently, Boyce (2008) has furthered what I might call the 'Hasluck/ McGarvie project' through the identification of four central themes

- the need for the role of the modern head of state to be given more serious attention than it has to date enjoyed in debates about the desirability of a republic
- the extent to which the conventions that constrain the immense formal gubernatorial powers might be codified (at least in part)
- the ways in which educational and other programs might heighten public awareness of the gubernatorial roles currently being played
- identification of the most appropriate mechanisms for the determination of continuing reforms and rationalisations (which would not necessarily lead to republican regimes).

To start with, Boyce favours a working party of governors' secretaries consulting closely with officials of chief ministers' departments and reporting to both a governors' conference and concerned cabinets.

Although these themes of Boyce's are valuable ones, he is on the whole fairly cautious in the reforms he advocates. So, when he turns to the exploration of his four themes and their implications, the limitations of his approach become manifest. Because he sticks so closely to current practices and orthodoxies, Boyce seldom allows himself the freedom to discuss reform proposals that go beyond such orthodoxies. For example, he accords little attention to experiences in those regimes—the semi-presidential—that have been growing greatly in numbers around the globe in recent decades and that can offer many important lessons for constitutional reformers in Westminster systems.

This limitation of Boyce's approach is most evident in 'Republicanism', the penultimate chapter of his book. Despite its title, *The Queen's Other Realms* gives authoritative support to mainstream Australian republican thinking. That mainstream has steadfastly clung to the merger assumption: that because the office of the head of state should be kept within minimalist bounds, its function should be discharged by a single officeholder, who would replace the current bicephalous arrangement. Although Boyce notes a serious tension between the 'twin roles' of constitutional guardian and symbol of national identity, he does not go on to consider the possibility that these roles should be performed by separate officeholders. In this respect, as in most others, he is firmly in the mainstream. Accordingly, he offers no criticism of the current strategy of the ARM, which is to force the electorate to choose between a number of 'models', all of them seriously flawed, in part because they all rest on the merger assumption.

One of the most important of Boyce's observations is his demonstration of the ways in which the traditional royal prerogative has in modern Westminster regimes been appropriated by political executives, to their very great empowerment. While he goes on to consider the ways in which residual head-of-state entitlements have allowed some sovereigns and their surrogates to play the limited Bagehotian roles of being consulted, and proffering warning and encouragement, he does not give as satisfactory an account as McGarvie previously did in his *Democracy* of the political economy of relations between heads of state and heads of government in Westminster regimes, and of the place of conventions in those political economies.

One pattern that has become increasingly apparent only in the months that have elapsed since the appearance of Boyce's book is that Australian Labor prime ministers are now selecting activist governors-general. Commenting on one of these, Sir William Deane, Boyce observes that his high profile 'is unlikely to be repeated'—a prediction that now is being challenged by the new Australian Governor-General, Quentin Bryce. We still lack a coherent account of the ways in which a modern governor might proceed. Some guidance can be obtained, however, from a perusal of Australia's leading student of the ethics of governance: John Uhr.

Uhr has extensively discussed republican writings in much of his work and has been closely associated with the NISA project, but has ignored the head of state in his most recent book, *Terms of Trust* (2005). Some valuable lessons can be learned from a comparison of the Uhr approach with that informing this monograph.

Uhr and I share commitments to parliamentary democracy, institutional integrity and republicanism. We differ in the degree of contingency that we are prepared to accept in the formulation of our respective reform strategies. Uhr does not question the central features of the power structures of Australian governance, such as the rigid disciplines of the parties or the orthodoxy of the three-branch division of powers. Instead, he is content to advance a number of modest but worthwhile reforms that make existing structures of dominance more accountable, without ultimately questioning their rationales (see, for example, the dozen recommendations with which he concludes his important 1998 work on deliberative democracy). As he observed later, 'policymaking is all about compromise' (Uhr 2005:39). At no point does he move on to a discussion of the topics that are at the centre of my reform proposals: the need for a collegial body to head up a monitory branch, in pursuit of many of the goals that Uhr covers under the rubric 'terms of trust'.

It will have become all too apparent by now that I favour the strengthening of positions that have long been underused—those relating to head-of-state offices. It is at this point, however, that I must attempt to resolve an issue that might seriously disturb the coherence of my argument. Long before I became interested in the problems arising from the threats to the integrity of the major institutions of governance and the need to proceed gradually on constitutional reform if we were to counter these threats, I belonged to the 'republic now' camp. And while I belonged in that camp, I had propounded a strategy for the immediate strengthening of head-of-state offices. While much of this strategy has had to be revised to make it consistent with my more recent indirect approach, a good deal of it remains in place. Therefore, I have decided to devote the next section of this monograph to an 'unpicking' of this strategy, before returning in the concluding section to a consideration of the ways in which the implementation of such a strategy could assist in the tackling of the major problems confronting advocates of fiducial governance.

3. Reconfiguring head-of-state offices in Australia

In this section, I advance eight propositions about the reform of gubernatorial offices in Australia. Taken together, these propositions constitute an ambitious, ultimately republican reform program. While there is a logical progression from one proposition to the next, the degree of political difficulty increases as we progress. So the extent to which the program can be implemented will vary from one jurisdiction to the next. Even if only the first proposition is accepted in a single jurisdiction, that would in itself represent a considerable initial reform. It would not, however, in itself guarantee a regime of fiducial governance. So, in the concluding section, I shall be taking as given the realisation of all eight propositions. In this way, I hope to demonstrate the ways in which the achievement of a fully republican regime could contribute to the remedying of the several regime defects identified in the preceding section.

a) Accountability of governors

Each governor should be more accountable than at present for what s/he does. Current arrangements continue to be excessively monarchical, in that governors are expected to regulate their own behaviour in accordance with the norms of what Peter Hennessy (1995) has dubbed the 'good chaps' culture characteristic of monarchical regimes.[1] Under the current arrangements, as long as the governor can keep happy the head of government (who is after all usually responsible for

---

1 Hennessy (1995) has pointed out that this culture is normally secretive. To the extent that we know anything about this culture, it comes from 'insiders' discussing what they have been cleared (or, as good chaps, have cleared themselves) to divulge. According to Hennessy (1995:56–7), at the core of the British arrangements is a 'golden triangle' of good chaps, consisting of the Queen's and the Prime Minister's Private Secretaries and the Cabinet Secretary. This triangle is not formally accountable to anyone else for much of what they do together, although they no doubt consult closely with their principals. They provide the best example, however, of the 'good chaps' culture especially typical of the monarchist regime. On the assumption that only good chaps make it to these high positions and are loyal to the service of 'the Crown', nothing more in the way of accountability is deemed to be required. And in Australia, the leading good chaps have been the governors themselves, as they have been chosen by their heads of government on criteria that are never made public. The activities of the 'good chaps' are of course regulated by conventions: 'the general agreements of public men about the "rules of the game" to be borne in mind in the conduct of public affairs' (Hennessy 1995:36–7). There is, however, usually a large measure of uncertainty about the current bindingness of any specific convention. Hennessy reports having been persuaded that any putative convention that could be abandoned by an incoming prime minister is not worthy of classification as a convention, no matter how many previous prime ministers have respected it. Yet some prime ministers are themselves uncertain about some of the conventions that should govern their own behaviour; Hennessy (1995:23) reports Baldwin's view that 'there may be one practice called "constitutional" which is falling into desuetude and there may be another practice which is creeping into use but is not yet constitutional'. Hence the preference for the judgments of 'good chaps' over the inflexibilities of formally stated constitutional rules.

his/her appointment) and (hopefully) the leader of the opposition as well, public accountability is deemed to have been satisfied. This bare-bones approach to the attainment of accountability is, however, dated and no longer applies to most public offices. Even in those areas where confidentiality must be maintained, experience in some of these other offices suggests ways in which gubernatorial accountability could be enhanced, without confidentiality being impaired.

Indeed, a useful distinction that can be drawn between the monarchist and the republican modes of governance is a cultural one. Cultural differences do affect the ways in which heads of state relate to heads of government, but the influence is an indirect one. The differences between republican and monarchical regimes are largely matters of style: the former are more open and place more clear and explicit institutional limitations on their heads of state than do the latter.[2] These differences do of course affect the nature of the relationships between the head of state and the head of government, but they do so in often delicate ways. Even republican regimes sometimes depend on good chaps when it comes to some affairs of state, but they do so reluctantly, as a last resort.

b) Gubernatorial position statements

Each governor should have a public 'job description' negotiated with his/ her head of government. Currently, the public has no way of knowing the full conception of the gubernatorial role held by an incumbent.[3] Often, the incumbent him/herself must test the public acceptability of his/her conception through the floating of 'trial balloons', which inevitably attract adverse comments from some parliamentarians. Such a state of affairs is quite unfair for incumbents. A couple of incumbents (McGarvie, Sir Guy Green) have made behind-the-scenes attempts to assess the extent to which governors around Australia have respected the constitutional counselling function pioneered 40 years ago by Hasluck, but these informal inquiries have fallen well short of the development of an explicit code of conduct.

Our comprehension of what our heads of state should do is shaped—usually tacitly—by our understanding of what States should do. The State is responsible for making exercises of differing kinds of authority—public and private— comprehensible to its citizens. When the head of state can do this, s/he is performing an expressive role: making sense of the ways in which authority is being exercised. Because much of this authority is exercised in conditions

---

2   Bagehot (1872:94) put the difference this way: 'Royalty will be strong because it appeals to diffused feeling; and Republics weak because they appeal to the understanding.'
3   I know of at least one recent governor who totally ignored the function of constitutional counselling, the importance of which is stressed here.

of confidentiality, this expressive role often has to take the form of vouching. Although most citizens are not allowed 'behind the scenes', the head of state can be there and can vouch for the integrity of what s/he has seen.

In a republic, an elected president would be responsible for vouching to interested publics that the arrangements for furthering institutional integrity were being properly balanced against those furthering responsiveness; an appointive governor would be responsible for the coordination, through the leadership of a governance review committee, of those myriad activities aimed at securing institutional integrity.

Accordingly, an important role is that of vouching to the citizenry that overall the integrity of our institutions is being satisfactorily balanced against the requirements of democratic responsiveness by the activities of our governors and other statutory officers (auditors- general, ombudsmen, and so on). This is not a role suitable for governors, for if they were responsible for such a role they would be in part vouching publicly for their own performance and would in any case be too close to the executive branch to be perceived by the citizenry as someone independently representing their interests in institutional integrity. A directly elected officer—a president—would be needed for the performance of this 'vouching' role.

As far as I am aware, ten years into the new millennium, no other contemporary republican democrat has yet begun theorising the developmental potentialities of the office of head of state. Only the monarchists have in recent years been celebrating that office, but their approach could hardly be described as developmental. It is quite the opposite; for the more intelligent monarchists, the lower the executive profile of the head of state, the better (Bogdanor 1995; Hennessy 1995).

Indeed, there is a curious bifurcation in the contemporary literature on heads of state. One would have expected that discussions of the roles of heads of state would have attended closely to theorisations of the modern state. Anyone who expected this would be seriously disappointed, for the treatments of heads of state (of which Boyce [2008] is an outstanding example) ignore the literature on the modern state, and those that deal with the nature of the modern state (of which Thompson [2001] can serve as an equally outstanding example)[4] ignore the roles of heads of state. Why should this be?

The short answer is that experiences in the twentieth century with heads of totalitarian states have so frightened us all (the outstanding statement of this condition of fright remains Cassirer [1963:ch. 18]) that we have considered

---

4   Although both Boyce and Thompson are political scientists, in the works cited they are working within very different traditions: formal constitutional arrangements and the pragmatics of statecraft, respectively.

it safest to adopt minimalist and formalist stances when confronting the inescapable need for heads of state. To engage in wider speculations about the development of new head-of-state roles has been considered altogether too dangerous. Yet it could turn out to be much more dangerous to attempt to sweep such considerations under the rug.

As Cassirer reminds us, the non-rational and symbolic dimensions of public life come to the fore at times of crisis. If we continue to shun the positive roles that our heads of state could perform in the fiducial governance of our modern states, we leave ourselves open to new totalitarian initiatives. It is much safer to consider openly the ways in which heads of state might be brought to play active but constrained roles in the securing of constitutionalist regimes around the globe.

c) Reviews of gubernatorial performance

Sir Paul Hasluck was Australia's first modern governor,[5] in that he set out to establish an ambitious gubernatorial counselling role:

> I tried to satisfy myself first that the [Executive] Council had the power under the Constitution or a statute to make the decision recommended, that the recommendation was made by competent authority and that any preliminary enquiry or other steps required by law had taken place…

> On matters which might be more controversial I would seek to satisfy myself that there was no conflict between the action recommended and any agreements, commitments or decisions of the government, and that respect had been paid to the conventions of the Constitution and the established procedures…

> I was also concerned with ensuring that there was no conflict among my advisers…If the subject matter obviously was of interest to several Ministers and departments I required an assurance that there had been interdepartmental consultation and that the recommendation was supported by all those directly concerned…if I saw a possible conflict of policy, I would ask whether or not a recommendation had been considered by Cabinet and, if not, would suggest that the Prime Minister should be asked for his direction whether it should go before Cabinet. (Hasluck 1979:38–9)[6]

---

5   Winterton (2004:43) supports the assessment of McGarvie that Hasluck was 'the founding architect of modern governorship in Australia'.

6   What is missing from this activist gubernatorial agenda is any explicit mention of the appropriateness of Executive actions under the Prerogatives power. Review of principles that should inform such actions would

Of course, this activist conception has proven controversial, with some governors (such as McGarvie) being strong supporters and others (such as Green) equally strong critics. Part of the reason for these differences of opinion might rest on variations in the performance of such bodies as cabinet offices. Even when such offices are performing well, it must, however, remain a gubernatorial responsibility to be satisfied that this has been happening.

So Hasluck's former political adversary, Gough Whitlam (1998:5), subsequently paid tribute to the value of the counsel that his government received from him. And a later governor-general, the formidable legal theorist Zelman Cowan (1985:142), went so far as to agree with Hasluck that the work 'demanded the highest intellectual and personal resources available to me'. It is hard to see what role other than that of constitutional counselling could have required the full intellectual resources of a mind such as Cowan's. Similarly, the equally formidable jurist Sir Henry Winneke 'found the constitutional side of the office interesting, satisfying and rewarding' (Coleman 1988:330). And McGarvie himself (1999:65, 68 ff.) provided an account of counselling—'a vital part of my role'—that has been very much in the Hasluckian tradition—one that seemed to be widely performed: 'From discussions, particularly at the annual Governors' Conferences, with those holding office in recent times, it is clear that the discreet but influential role personified by Sir Paul Hasluck is now widely followed in Australia' (McGarvie 1999:26).[7]

Despite McGarvie's impressions, by no means all Australian governors have trod the Hasluck path. An early modifier was Governor-General Sir Ninian Stephen. Galligan (1991:69–70) reports that '[b]y Sir Ninian Stephen's time this [Hasluckian] watchdog function had been largely replaced by procedures designed to ensure that matters coming to the Executive Council have been properly dealt with by the appropriate government Ministers and law offices'.

Nevertheless, even after much of the quality of the work had been enhanced by cabinet offices and the like, a gubernatorial responsibility should have remained—that of satisfying him/herself that the quality of the work done was at an acceptable level.

Another former governor, Sir Guy Green, has subsequently produced an elegant elaboration of the position of his fellow former judge Stephen. Green identifies three models of the gubernatorial role: (Hasluckian) interventionism; the 'benign mentor' (unsurprisingly, Green's favoured model); and the 'mechanical idiot' (which Green rejects 'fairly summarily', although it should be noted that

---

be an important concern of each Council of State.

7 This is an excellent example of the 'good chaps' mystique still enveloping the gubernatorial office. Nothing as vulgar as an empirical study of the practices of governors appears to be possible; the public must be satisfied with the retrospective impressions of one former governor!

at least one recent governor appears to have conformed to this model).[8] Green does, however, give qualified support to McGarvie's impressions. Reporting on an informal survey of governors that he conducted in the late 1990s, Green (2006b) noted that '[g]overnors or the Secretariats of Executive Councils in Australia do in practice exercise an effective monitoring function by raising significant queries with the Ministers or departments presenting items to the Council. In some jurisdictions this occurs "very frequently". It remains unclear, however, just how the majority of governors distributed themselves between the interventionist and the benign mentor models. Indeed, one well-placed observer has gone so far as to claim that the distinction is now 'a distinction without a difference' (Smith 2005:161). Whether or not this is an accurate criticism, an important issue remains, for it is yet to be determined just what should be the boundaries of gubernatorial concern with the activities of the executive branch.

If a Hasluckian constitutional counsellor role is deemed appropriate, a governance review council/committee should regularly assess performance in this role. On Hasluck's own account of this role presented above, it nicely complements that of the ombudsman, with the governor protecting institutional integrity at the political level and the ombudsman doing so at the administrative level. A governor who played this role could thus be accorded membership of the governance review council/committee the creation of which in each of our nine jurisdictions was recommended by the NISA project.

d) The need for a council of state

If a governance review council/committee were to be responsible for work of such political sensitivity, it would need to be protected by a body such as the Irish Council of State. While the NISA report recognised the need for political champions to take up the reforms it was recommending, none has yet appeared, and such champions are highly likely to remain absent while our style of partisan politics remains unreformed. The introduction of a council of state (with a membership along Irish lines) could begin to discipline our parties in new ways, for such bodies would offer new pathways of advancement for the more consensually minded of our political leaders.

Councils of state are curious chameleon-like bodies. All states that differentiate heads of state from heads of government—and they are a considerable majority in the modern world—possess some such body to handle relations between these two centres of authority. None, however, has yet emerged to take a leading role in securing the integrity of all the major institutions of governance. Some,

---

8   As each governor still remains free to define the role as s/he pleases, it would be unfair to identify the one who on my information conforms to the 'mechanical idiot' model.

such as the British Privy Council, have fallen into desuetude;[9] others, such as the French *Conseil d'Etat*, have become specialised in one area of governance (in the French case, constitutional and administrative law). And some, such as the Irish Council of State, have been designed to exercise very little authority. Nevertheless, the Irish Council of State possesses a membership that is well suited to the securing of institutional integrity at the highest levels, for it brings together the heads of the three recognised branches, together with a wide range of community representatives.[10]

In the Australian case, it might be objected that we already possess our own variations on the privy council theme, in the executive councils that exist in each jurisdiction. These councils have, however, in modern times become so captured by our partisan systems that it is impossible to envisage them playing a broad fiducial governance role. Since the Hasluck innovations, however, they all possess the potentiality of supporting a governor with strong interests in the integrity of government programs.

In approaching these tasks of fiduciality assurance, councils of state will benefit from their composition as collegial bodies. As Baylis (1989)[11] suggests, such bodies are particularly well suited to the furtherance of two of the ideals that Ackerman proposes for a regime of constrained parliamentarianism: democratic governance and integrity of public institutions. Indeed, the widening of the scope of our inquiry from the '-cracy' on which Baylis focuses (his entire analysis rests on a fundamental distinction between collegiality and monocratic leadership) to one that encompasses '-archy' (as in the above distinction between monarchical and polyarchical regimes) allows us to move beyond the findings of Baylis. Take,

---

9   Over many years, the Privy Council served as a model for many constitutional designers. For example, it provided a model for the Australian executive councils that are discussed below. More spectacularly, the American founding fathers vested the famous 'advise and consent' powers in the Senate in the hope that this might encourage it to emulate the House of Lords as the seat of some of the powers of the Privy Council (Sundquist 1992:37, 61, 313).

10   The membership of the Irish Council of State is as follows: Prime Minister; Deputy Prime Minister; Chief Justice; President of the High Court; Presiding Officers of the two Houses of Parliament; Attorney-General; any former president, prime minister or chief justice willing to serve; up to seven presidential nominees. For reasons stated elsewhere in this monograph, it would be highly desirable to grant leaders of the opposition seats on each council of state. Republican reformers have been slow to perceive the great potential of the Irish arrangements—which were after all fashioned in the 1930s by a great statesman confronting a situation not unlike our own—because they have assumed that the current bicephalous arrangement that we possess must disappear, so that we would have a single officer, a president, as head of state. As the Irish President does not have the authority to perform the functions of Australian governors, her office and the Council of State that supports it have been incorrectly deemed irrelevant to Australia (see Power 2005, 2006).

11   Baylis's (1989:9–10) important work is explicitly concerned only with executive branches. Nevertheless, the work throws much light on the strengths and weaknesses of collegial ways of proceeding, and this light can assist us to deepen our understanding of how a collegial body that headed up an integrity branch should proceed. The most important lesson is one that carries a strong caution. Collegial bodies are particularly well suited to the tackling of technically complex problems that require heavy support from specialised bureaucracies, especially those embedded in influential policy communities. This is all very well, but the synergies that link collegial deliberative bodies and their bureaucrat officials strengthen a tendency that both usually exhibit strongly: a tendency to secrecy and insensitivity to outside criticism.

for example, his characterisation of monocratic leadership as being one mainly of symbolic reassurance (not unlike the role that used to be claimed for heads of state). When we consider the function of symbolic reassurance within the wider framework of a polyarchical regime, we can see that the function breaks down into two quite distinct parts: direct and indirect. When a head of government provides direct reassurance, s/he is referring to the performance of institutions under his/her direct control. When a head of state provides indirect assurance, s/he is vouching for the integrity of the institutions involved, many of which are not under his/her direct control.

e) Public 'vouching' for the integrity of council of state processes

The task of publicly vouching for the integrity of the work of these collegial bodies should not be the responsibility of any of the 'working members'. If the proposed new bodies were to earn reputations for trustworthiness, they would need to have spokespeople who could regularly vouch for the integrity of their proceedings. And, if allegations of conflicts of interest were to be avoided, such spokespeople should be independent of those whose work was being vouched for. An independent chair of a council of state would be well suited to this task.

f) Directly elected 'voucher'

If public trust in these new institutional arrangements were to be optimised, the 'voucher' would need to be directly elected. A publicly elected 'voucher' could appropriately be dubbed 'president'. If the new institutional arrangements came to be widely seen as helping to increase public trust in our institutions of governance, the spokesperson would probably have to be elected. In the Australian federal system, it could well turn out to be the case that the national president could come to chair several (or even all) of the state/territory councils of state as well. If this were to happen, a more effective form of federalism could emerge. There would certainly be sufficient work to justify the continuation of a strengthened bicephalous configuration of head-of-state roles.

g) Two forms of politics

Although many of the more perceptive writers on democratic governance have differentiated two forms of politics—a 'lower' and a 'higher'—the fundamental distinction made by Thompson (2001) best suits the purposes of this monograph. Her characterisation of the 'masculine principle' of politics closely resembles that of partisan contestation in Australia—one that 'employs power, with reason, to meet immediate objectives'. The 'feminine principle', on the other hand, 'is attached to traditions that maintain the strength of social affection across communities…It is linked with creativity, the unconscious, interiorization and mystery' (Thompson 2001:103)[12]. This differentiation is valuable in the present context,[13] for it asserts that both 'principles'—in the terms used throughout this monograph: the partisan and the fiducial—are essential to good governance, for they function 'in a distinctive equilibrium and [are] dependent upon maintaining a fine balance' (Thompson 2001:102).

Such a 'feminine' president would not be, as is frequently asserted, apolitical or 'above' politics, but would be involved in a form of politics different from the partisan form that decides the composition of the government of the day. The boundaries between the two forms of government would have to be negotiated— and continually renegotiated—in the council of state. The mainstream view that the head of state should be 'above' politics stems from fears that a directly elected head might challenge the head of government on major policies (Power 2008a). While this is undoubtedly an important issue, it is one that now confronts every one of the 'semi-presidential' regimes—about one-quarter of all the national regimes in the contemporary world (Elgie 2004; Elgie and Moestrup 2007, 2008).[14] Some of these regimes—such as the half-dozen that have developed 'corrective' head-of-state roles not unlike those introduced into Australia by Hasluck (Siaroff 2003)—should offer some relevant lessons for us.[15]

---

12   From a quite different feminist direction, Eisler (1987: 105) has introduced the term 'gylany', which bears strong resemblances to Thompson's conception of balance.

13   On one perceptive reading of Ackerman (Choudhry and Mount 2006), a similar distinction—between 'normal' and 'constitutive' politics—is made by him, and is, as is argued in this monograph, central to his rationale for serial referenda.

14   There is one important lesson for comparative governance studies that should be noted here. Writing two decades ago, just before the explosion in the number of semi-presidential regimes, even so capable a scholar as Baylis was dismissive of the importance of such regimes. Admittedly, he devoted considerable attention to the French Fifth Republic, which he was content to classify as presidential. The only other regime of this nature to receive even the slightest attention was Finland, which Baylis (1989:128) passed over as an uninteresting 'hybrid'.

15   On 17 April 2008, I published an article in the Melbourne *Age*, in which I identified these regimes: Ireland, Finland, Lithuania, Poland, Bulgaria and Macedonia. The article attracted no interest. The surprising lack of Australian interest in semi-presidential regimes continues. In the just published volume *The Australian Study of Politics* (Rhodes 2009), I am the only one of 37 contributors to mention such regimes. This paucity of citing of course reflects the lack of interest in the wider political science community, so that the eminent comparatist Leslie Holmes (2009) does not mention these regimes in his characteristically thorough survey of Australian contributions to his specialty.

h) A pathway to the republic

The development of the two separate roles of constitutional counsellor and of 'voucher' would continue the current bicephalous practices, but would do so in ways that offered a politically feasible pathway to a republic. As long as the republican movement remains divided between the selectionists (who value most highly the constitutional counselling work that has been performed by at least some of our governors) and the direct electionists (who favour a presidential conception of the office of head of state), the attainment of the republic will probably continue to elude us. It is only when each side is given what they most value that the passage of a referendum on the republic could begin to appear feasible.

4. Conclusion: republican measures for a republican future

For forms of government let fools contest
Whate'er is best administer'd is best

— Alexander Pope

Elegant in its cynicism as this couplet is, it ultimately fails, because the quality of administration usually depends in significant part on the nature of the form of government—the regime—under which it functions.

Because of the ubiquity of imputation, the republican mode of governing is always difficult. The republican might succeed in making explicit some long-tacit norm, only to find it slipping back into another assumptive world. Take, for example, the phenomenon of regulation, which is always a concern of governments, but a concern that has moved to centre stage in the contemporary world according to one recent perceptive account (Braithwaite 2008). After some time considering the phenomenon of modern regulation to be best approached under the rubric 'the regulatory state', Braithwaite now deems it more appropriate to allow the State to recede into the background of regulatory capitalism. Why? Because governments are now politically pressured to regulate the activities of their own agencies (Braithwaite 2008:21), and many activities are being regulated by global bodies with remits wider than any nation-state. So, Braithwaite argues, it is no longer appropriate to have a core governance definition focused on the nation-state.

In this, of course, Braithwaite differs sharply from Keane, with his core concept of monitory democracy. To place capitalism at the centre of the definitional field is, however, to marginalise fiducial political action—the performance of governance that provides a genuine basis for strong and continuing public trust. Braithwaite is after all not averse to endorsing institutional untidiness,[1] for this can provide opportunities for 'interstitial freedom': the phenomenon that can be observed when the citizenry uncovers openings for free action in the interstices of governing institutions—openings that were not intended by the designers of those institutions. While no liberal republican can be hostile to interstitial freedom—for we all deserve all the breaks that come our way in the modern world—s/he cannot be content with the solely accidental and the

---

1 At one point, he expresses a preference for 'many semi-autonomous powers recursively checking one another, rather than a few autonomous branches of governance' (Braithwaite 1997:312).

contingent as bases for fiducial governance. Such governance does require our
very best efforts in institutional design. Freedom that is based on such design
work is more secure than the interstitial form.

In this concluding section of the monograph, then, I am unashamedly political
in my arguments. I shall take it as a given that a jurisdiction has proceeded well
down my order of institutional reform set out in the preceding section. In this
way, I hope to show most clearly the ways in which a fully republican regime
could effectively tackle the tasks of fiducial governance. I shall therefore be
working my way through the problems identified in Section 2, but doing so in
reverse order, so that I shall be able to conclude with a discussion of the ways
in which a republican version of the regime of constrained parliamentarianism
could strengthen our democracy.[2]

Armed with the set of new and rejuvenated institutional mechanisms introduced
in the preceding section, we can now return to the components of the expanded
framework of constrained parliamentarianism. This time, however, we can be
much briefer, for as they are presently constituted, the several components
share the relatively small number of problems that would be ameliorated by the
introduction of these new mechanisms.

a) Viable role for a contemporary head of state

To place the roles of a contemporary head of state in the context of constrained
parliamentarianism is to identify clearly the unsuitability of the monarchical
style of governing. If a regime is to be able to respond fully to the demands of
polyarchical rule, it needs to demonstrate the capacity to handle 'multi-valued
choices' (Stewart 1974). Because of its distinctively different politics, a council
of state would be able to develop this capacity in ways well beyond the reach of
partisan contestation.

In further developing this capacity for fiducial politics, each council of state
would be building on the work that has been accomplished over the years as
our parliaments have struggled to establish viable committee systems, for these
often display a consensual politics close to the fiducial. Indeed, over time the
activities of a council of state could have the effect of strengthening still more
the committee systems of its parliament, because of the ways in which it will
be softening the nature of partisan contestation and indeed changing the very
nature of our parties. As this transformation of our parties continued, the council

---

2   In a companion monograph that I am preparing with Harshan Kumarasingham, we shall be arguing that
the constitutional reforms that are most feasible in the foreseeable future in New Zealand could fall well short
of republicanism.

of state could be expected to withdraw in the face of stronger parliamentary committee work. It is in the very nature of fiducial governance that the head-of-state roles are not primarily those of doing, but rather of assuring him/herself that appropriate action is being taken somewhere in the system of governance. As the Hasluck approach considered above indicates, the holder of a head–of-state office has only to intervene directly when s/he discerns faults in the performance of others.

It could be expected that each council of state would take its lead from its head-of-state leaders and would be equally circumspect in respecting the integrity of the other branches of governance whose representatives would of course be participating in its deliberations.

b) Serial referenda

If the proposed councils of state were to commit themselves to the principles of serial referenda on matters of high fiducial policy, the whole culture of constitutional reform in Australia could be transformed. If referendum proposals were to be generated by fiducially minded partisan leaders meeting in collegial deliberations, the citizenry could be expected to view them more favourably than it has in the past, when reform proposals were generated for the most part by remote commissions of lawyers. And if the serial nature of these referendum exercises were to be institutionalised along the lines recommended by Ackerman, their very familiarity could enhance their prospects of success.

c) Integrity of major institutions

The reform program here proposed provides answers to the two questions that have most perplexed the advocates of greater integrity in our institutions of governance. The first of these is the discovery of political champions. For the reasons already stated, these are unlikely to emerge from our current, unreformed democratic regime. A directly elected president would, however, be well placed to perform the champion's role. The second question is the identification of those who would be well placed to undertake the work of comprehensive regime design. As we have seen, the governance review councils/committees proposed by the integrity advocates would have too narrow a brief to be able to undertake reviews of governance arrangements *tout court*. For this work of comprehensive review to be undertaken, the much more broadly constituted councils of state that I recommend would be admirably suited.

With these arrangements firmly in place, the reformed regime would be well equipped to deal creatively with the problem that is always the most vexing for any democratic regime: how to devise extra-constitutional practices that can overcome the policy rigidities caused by the intersection of the formalisms of constitutional phrasing, on the one hand, and the inflexibilities of partisan contestation, on the other.

When the head of government and the leader of the opposition are required to negotiate the scope of partisan contestation in a collegial setting oriented towards fiduciality, it becomes possible for that same collegial body to work on the overall design of the regime's constitutional arrangements.

d) Securing human rights

While the dialogue model of securing human rights through a charter is an attractive one, in none of the regimes that has adopted this model has collegial dialogue been attained. And the reason for this lacuna is clear enough. Only in the setting provided by a properly constituted council of state could the dialogues essential to the charter model of securing human rights be conducted.

The awkwardness inevitably associated with the functions of the attorney-general—attempting to perform non-partisan functions in a context of continuing partisan contestation—would be removed. Indeed, in some jurisdictions, it could be deemed appropriate to seat this officer (and possibly his/her shadow as well) on the council of state—a context for the discharge of his/her long-established quasi- judicial functions that would avoid the difficulties caused by partisan rigidities.

As the listing of current deficiencies discussed above clearly indicates, the design of a regime that reconciled the need for human rights to be entrenched in ways that respected the ultimate role of the Parliament in determining the scope of those rights is one that typically falls short because of the rigidities of partisan contestation. The reformed regime here recommended would provide a way through such difficulties, for it would be the fiducial politics of the council of state, rather than the partisan politics of the Executive, that would determine the design of the human rights regime. Party leaders would continue to play the leading roles in this work, but they would do so in a collegial setting that would impose new, but more flexible, disciplines on them. In such a setting, strong differences of opinion would continue to express themselves, with conservatives opposed to progressives on the definition of the proper scope of the rights to be protected (social and economic as well as political and civil?), but issues such as these would be settled in each jurisdiction away from the rigidities of partisanship.

Along this dimension of constrained parliamentarianism, a distinctively new style of problem tackling—what we could term dialoguing—would emerge as each council of state wrestled with the design of a fiducial regime that genuinely respected human rights.

e) Independent judiciary

Under this heading we encounter an apparent paradox. Surely, it could be objected, the involvement of the judiciary in the politics of a council of state would compromise the independence of the judiciary? The answer to this important question is most conveniently phrased as follows: if the representatives of the judiciary were able to participate in deliberations about the boundaries around partisan contestation that should be observed, this would make it not more but less likely that the judiciary might in the future find itself in the middle of partisan disputes. And the office of head of state would be much better suited to act as the guardian of judicial independence than the attorney-general, whose partisan commitments might continue seriously to weaken his/her capacity to act in this way.

We could expect considerable variation between jurisdictions in the ways in which the leaders of the judicial branch decided to handle their representation in the council of state. Some, like their Irish colleagues,[3] would be relaxed about direct participation;[4] others might prefer to be represented by surrogates, such as retired judges, who could regularly consult with current officeholders.

This discussion has introduced a further important dimension to the work of the proposed councils of state: the boundaries of the dialoguing activity would have to be negotiated—and continually renegotiated—in ways that respected the integrity of the established roles of those coming from other branches and from civil society. As I note in the Appendix, a recent Senate Committee report (Parliament of Australia 2009b) could provide firm grounds for the establishment of a new body (which I have tentatively called a judicial selection and protection committee of a council of state). Such a body would be well placed to address the issues as the political dimensions of inter-branch dialogue.

---

3 And in New South Wales? In that jurisdiction, the activist Chief Justice has been strongly advocating a stronger judicial role in the securing of institutional integrity (Spigelman 2004, 2005).

4 According to the foremost authority on Australian constitutional law, such representation would ultimately require constitutional change to be in order (Zines 2008: 262 — on judges appointed as *personae designatae*). In the meantime, until the climate for constitutional reform improved, the views of the judiciary might best be presented by retired judges serving on councils of state, although serving judges with strong personal interests in broad issues of governance could well participate.

f) Professional public service

A similar point can be made under this heading. While the head of the public service in each jurisdiction is well suited to protect the integrity of the public service, s/he needs high-level collegial support in discharging this heavy responsibility. While much of this collegial support would be provided by the proposed merit and equity committee of the council of state, the council itself— and its presidential leader—would be able to provide the democratic legitimacy needed to underpin the deliberations of the committee.

g) Strong upper house

Of all the institutions that will be affected by the proposed reform program, this is the one whose future shape will be most unpredictable, because the most powerful influences on it will be indirect. The involvement of the parties in the head-of-state election campaigns will transform them and in the process shift the balance between the styles of politics characteristic of the two chambers— and will shift the balance very much in the direction of the upper house style.

In Australia, the Senate has distinguished itself in the past four decades through its development of the most impressive committee system of any of our parliaments. It has been able to do this because it has for most of that time not been under the control of the governing party. Its further development over the next four decades could be heavily shaped by the emergence of a regime of fiducial governance, for such an emergence would open up new areas of investigation and policy development free of the stranglehold of partisan contestation.

h) Federal structure

There is one important assumption that Galligan shared with every other writer of the 1990s that should at this point be again questioned. This is the 'merger assumption', which uncritically posits that the current bicephalous arrangement (monarch *plus* governor) should be replaced with a single office. What, however, if we come to agree that a) the gubernatorial role that was developed by Hasluck and subsequently celebrated by former governor McGarvie is valuable and should be retained and indeed strengthened; and b) the wider community role currently being attempted by the monarchical head of state should be developed in ways that would make it most appropriate for a directly elected leader to perform it?

Such a leader would be well placed to introduce processes of serial referenda, along the lines recommended by Ackerman. The justification of our federal system would be much stronger if the experience of referenda on constitutional reform were to take a turn in a more positive direction. At present, as we have seen, champions of an Australian federal republic such as Galligan have had to place too much trust in positive referenda results of long ago.

While the reforms proposed will have a rejuvenating influence on the Australian federal system, the roles that the president might play in state/territory jurisdictions will vary. In the president's home state, it would be most likely that the Commonwealth pattern of gubernatorial constitutional counselling and presidential vouching would be replicated. In other jurisdictions, however, different arrangements might be needed. In some, the president might be able to nominate an agent—such as the chairperson of an important parliamentary committee or the presiding officer of an upper house.—to perform the vouching function. In others, especially where the constitutional counselling function was securely established in a cabinet secretariat, the gubernatorial incumbent might be entrusted with the vouching function.

It is at this juncture that the councils of state would encounter the institution with which the most important jurisdictional issues would have to be negotiated: the executive branch-oriented Council of Australian Governments. Just as the head of government and the leader of the opposition would be expected in each council of state to negotiate (and continually renegotiate) the boundaries of partisan contestation in that jurisdiction, so representatives of the councils of state and of Australian governments would have to engage in parallel negotiations and renegotiations, quite possibly through each council's sectoral peak bodies chamber.

A genuine differentiation of the realms of partisan and fiducial politics, of the kind that could be delivered through councils of state, would permit the systematic development of coherent intergovernmental programs. It could even result in the better integration of the 'dual constitutional culture' (Galligan 1995:50), for it would facilitate the determination of those programs that could be freed of the heavier constraints of partisan contestation. Much heavy intergovernmental negotiation would remain, but it would be coordinated by the several new monitory branches through their respective councils of state.

i) Parliamentary democracy

The insertion of a democratically elected president into a regime of constrained parliamentarianism would for the first time allow intelligible coordination to be achieved among the several constraints operating on the Executive. In this way, the accountability of a parliamentary-based executive would be strengthened, and with it the trustworthiness of all the major institutions of governance. Democracy (in its widely accepted Schumpeterian sense[5]) is essential to any form of effective governance in the contemporary world, but it could be rejuvenated in a regime of fiducial governance. The recognition of another form of democratic politics—to sit alongside but ultimately to defer to the familiar partisan form—could rejuvenate our parties. If the parties came to be seen as central participants in fiducial politics, they would become much more attractive to those whose interests were not those that readily lent themselves to partisan regimentation and contestation. (While this transformation of our parties would have the most immediate consequences for our upper houses and their committees, which I have noted above, in the longer term they would also begin to exercise beneficial influences on lower houses and their committee systems as well.)

With the establishment of councils of state in each of our jurisdictions, then, new balances will be struck in the ways in which representative democracy relates to fiducial governance. The deliberations of each of these councils will provide leadership for each monitory branch. Through these deliberations, the dialogues essential to the integrity of our major institutions and to the protection of basic human rights will be effectively conducted. Because these dialogues will establish firm boundaries around the fields of partisan disputation, judges and senior public servants will be able to participate in these dialogues without placing their independence in jeopardy. The institutions most beset by partisan contestation—sub-national governments and upper houses—will find more effective ways of coordinating their fiducial activities, while retaining the capacity of serving as arenas for vigorous partisan debate, all the more vigorous because it will be more clearly focused.

---

5   Schumpeter (1954:269) defined democracy as follows: 'An institutional arrangement for arriving at political decisions in which individuals acquire the power to decide by means of a competitive struggle for the people's vote'

Appendix

A consolidated council of state agenda listing[1]

While each council of state will have to develop its own distinctive agenda, none will be able to avoid the following set of issues that are especially close to the cause of fiducial governance. It should be recognised, however, that much work would have to be done before this could begin to address any of these items. It is for this reason that it would be prudent to begin with an interim committee (as recommended in Note 1 on this page).

For example, the very functions of the council might well be shaped by its foundation membership (and vice versa) and some of these membership issues would most appropriately be considered after the heads of state and of government had convened initial exploratory meetings of interests likely to figure prominently in the work of the constituent chambers (which would number three if, as suggested above, the lead of the Indigenous community were to be followed).

Were any government to pursue seriously the strategy I have here recommended, the constitutional consequences would of course ultimately be considerable. No government, however, should be too quickly deterred from taking the first steps, for the full implementation of my reform program would take many years. All I am here trying to do is set forth a sense of long-term direction for the ways our governments might reform themselves. I have been encouraged in this enterprise by the acute observation of one well-placed observer, John Uhr (2009:132), who recently commented on the 'remarkably adaptive Australian parliamentary system'.

Agenda item 1: functions of the council

Form and coordinate the activities of the council's several specialist committees.

Provide a forum for determination of the scope of partisan political competition.

---

1   In the interests of simplicity, I have throughout this monograph referred to 'councils of state' as though they were already established. In practice, of course, agreement-in-principle to proceed, which had been reached between a governor and head of government, would be followed initially by the establishment of a working group or interim committee to work on such topics as those covered under the first two headings in the listing below. Any decisions taken by these interim bodies would, however, have to be ratified by the council of state at its first meeting, so I consider my simplification justified.

Comment

One reason why each interim committee would find the three-chambers structure attractive would be their suitability for engaging in wide-ranging consultations to identify those functions that were central to citizen perceptions of the nature of fiducial governance. Some of the more obvious functions—each to be developed by an appropriate committee—are listed below.

Agenda item 2: membership of the council

Comment

Those councils that had decided to follow the lead recently provided by Indigenous interests and adopted the three-chamber structure would have to move on to determine (at least on an interim basis) the composition of constituent chambers.

I have above indicated some of the interests that should be considered for inclusion in the three national chambers

- chamber 1: national peak bodies (representatives from the three established branches of government, from the National Congress of Australia's First Peoples)
- chamber 2: sectoral peak bodies (representatives from the Council of Australian Governments)
- chamber 3: local community and individual representatives (representatives from the Australian Collaboration—see Section 1(i above—and from organisations representing interests not specifically covered by the Collaboration (for example, women, the aged, the disabled[2]).

In approaching the issues surrounding its own composition and structure, the interim committee for the council of state will have to discriminate between those institutions that are obvious inclusions (such as the representatives of the three established branches of governance) and those that would probably be included (which might need to be reviewed before a decision could be taken on the nature of its representation).[3]

---

2 Some of the interests formally represented under one of the 'umbrellas' of the Australian Collaboration might require separate consideration eg the Muslim community, from which a persuasive case for an Islamic constitutionalism rooted in the realm of the sacred has recently emerged (Aly 2007).

3 A good example of this latter 'contingent' category would be the Council of the Order of Australia. Although this council (and the awards it recommended) were restructured in modern times, so that knighthoods were no longer bestowed, it retained many characteristics that were more suitable to a monarchical than a republican regime. The structure of its awards closely reflect the class structure, with those of the highest status being reserved for 'good chaps'; excessive secrecy surrounds its decision-making processes; and its lack of public accountability means that the severe biases its awards display are never publicly debated. The citizenry has never had much say in the affairs of the council; the awards descend on the population twice a year with

It would be relatively straightforward for any interim committee operating at the state/territory level to modify these arrangements to suit their particular circumstances. For example, one or more of the established branches could bid to take over parts of the monitory function (for a bid of this kind emanating from a legislative branch, see Griffith 2005).

Agenda item 3: committee 1 of the council— governance review committee

Comment

This of course is a body similar to that recommended by the NISA project. It is here presented, however, as a committee and not a council, for it would draw the needed political champions from the council of state, of which it would be one of the principal committees. It could well turn out in many jurisdictions to be the *primus inter pares* of the committees, for its concerns would lie at the heart of fiducial governance. To take a most important field, this Committee would have the responsibility of developing recommendations for its Council of State on the rules and standards, if any, that should constrain the exercise of prerogative powers by the Executive.

Agenda item 4: committee 2 of the council—human rights charter review committee

Comment

In this committee, on which representatives of all three of the established branches would be especially keen to be represented, the necessary inter-branch dialogue—called for but not made adequate provision for in all regimes that have to date established charter arrangements—would begin. Such dialogue would of course continue in the deliberations of each of the councils of state.

Agenda item 5: committee 3 of the council—judicial selection and protection committee

Comment

The 1997 *Statement of Independence* of the Australian Chief Justices—which impressed Patapan (2000:167) as 'remarkable' but unclear in its provenance—

---

precious little impact. It is time that the need for awards is reviewed and, if their continuation is deemed desirable, a major exercise of public consultation should precede the taking of decisions on the future structure of awards.

provides ample justification for the establishment of such a collegial body, which might in time morph into a judicial services commission: 'To enable the judiciary to achieve its objectives and perform its functions, it is essential that judges be chosen on the basis of proven competence, integrity and independence' (Chief Justices of Australia 1997).

In some societies, the appointment of judges by, with the consent of or after consultation with, a judicial services commission has been seen as a means of ensuring that those chosen judges are appropriate for the purpose. Where a judicial services commission is adopted, it should include representatives from the higher judiciary and the independent legal profession as a means of ensuring that judicial competence, integrity and independence are maintained.

In the absence of a judicial services commission, the procedures for the appointment of judges should be clearly defined and formalised and information about them should be available to the public.

Indeed, a Senate Committee has very recently argued along similar—indeed rather republican—lines:

> The committee recommends that when the appointment of a federal judicial officer is announced the Attorney-General should make public the number of nominations and applications received for each vacancy.

> If the government or department prepared a short-list of candidates for any appointment, the number of people on the list should also be made public.

> The committee recommends that the process for appointments to the High Court should be principled and transparent. The committee recommends that the Attorney-General should adopt a process that includes advertising vacancies widely and should confirm that selection is based on merit and should detail the selection criteria that constitute merit for appointment to the High Court.

> The committee recommends that the Commonwealth government establish a federal judicial commission modelled on the Judicial Commission of New South Wales. (Parliament of Australia 2009b)

Agenda item 6: committee 4 of the council—public service merit and equity committee

Comment

Establishment of this collegial body would give belated recognition to the two-decades-old recommendations of the report of the Review of Public Service

Personnel Management in Victoria. As the much more recent argument of Podger (2007) indicates, such a collegial presence is sorely needed at the apex of each of our regimes. Only through the effective functioning of such bodies could citizen trust in our public services be restored.

Agenda item 7: committee 5 of the council—honours and awards committee

Comment

Clearly, the new councils would share important interests with the existing Council for the Order of Australia. Whether the existing Council for the Order of Australia should be reconstituted as a committee of the national council of state will be a controversial issue best left without further comment in this monograph (see Note 3 of this Section). It should be noted, however, that honours are important to any conception of fiducial politics 'for what they signal about the values and good works that matter' (Braithwaite 2008:125). And sometimes those who should be honoured are those usually shunned by established honours councils, such as those non-partisans who have stimulated a measure of public controversy in their pursuit of public values.

Agenda item 8: committee 6 of the council— deliberative chambers committee

Comment

Some years ago, I persuaded the Commission on Constitutional Reform in Victoria that it was desirable for the members of the newly reconstituted upper house (the Legislative Council) to form regional committees on which they would deliberate with municipal representatives and other community figures.[4] Unsurprisingly, the government of Steve Bracks ignored this recommendation. In this new context, however, such an arrangement could with benefit be modified for introduction at the national and state/territory levels. For example, senators and municipal councillors who were able to secure seats on their respective state/territory councils of state would be especially well placed to serve as linkages between the differing spheres of governance.

---

4   See the 2002 report of the Constitution Commission Victoria: *A House for Our Future* (p. 51).

Agenda item 9: committee 7 of the council— interrelations between councils of state, and determining the role of the national head of state in activities of the council

Comment

While it would be up to each council of state to determine the role it would like the national head of state to play in its deliberations, this would be an issue of considerable interest to the national council and the head of state him/herself. It is not inconceivable that the councils in some jurisdictions would make provision for a new 'vouching' officer, such as the chairperson of an important parliamentary committee or the presiding officer of an upper house. If this were to occur, the relations of such an officer with the national-level 'voucher'—the president—would need to be carefully negotiated between the councils concerned.

Another important responsibility that could be placed on this committee would be that of developing recommendations on the development of proper relations between Australian councils and international bodies.[5] Once fiducially oriented councils of state came into existence (either through institutional innovation, as would have to be the case in Australia, or through the reorientation of existing councils, as in many existing semi-presidential regimes), they would naturally seek to establish linkages with other similarly oriented councils. Although such interactions would become evident first at regional levels, it would not be long before their relevance to global concerns would come under the attention of bodies such as the United Nations. While this is a topic that I shall take up in the companion essay, it is one that will increasingly demand the attention of governance practitioners long after I have departed the scene.

Agenda item 10: design of the reform program

Design the constitutional reform program, with particular attention to the sequencing of proposals to be submitted to the citizenry through serial referenda.

Comment

While much worthwhile work can be accomplished before constitutional reforms are attempted, ultimately popular referenda will be needed. The approach of governance leaders will, however, be far from minimalist orthodoxy, for they

---

5   This important issue is treated at somewhat greater length in the epilogue to the companion essay.

will welcome public deliberation on a sequence of reform proposals. They will be fortified by the knowledge that their commitment to the fiducial cause will have become publicly known well before the first referendum tests are faced.

References

Ackerman, Bruce 1998, *We the People 2: Transformations*, The Belknap Press of Harvard University Press, Cambridge, Mass.

Ackerman, Bruce 2000, 'The new separation of powers', *Harvard Law Review*, vol. 113, no. 3 (January), pp. 633–729.

Ackerman, Bruce 2005, *The Failure of the Founding Fathers: Jefferson, Marshall and the rise of presidential democracy*, The Belknap Press of Harvard University Press, Cambridge, Mass.

Ackerman, Bruce 2007, '2006 Oliver Wendell Holmes Lecture: the living constitution', *Harvard Law Review*, vol. 120 (May), pp. 1737–812.

Addison, Joseph 1712, 'Spectator no. 287', in Henry Morley (ed.), *The Spectator*, Routledge, London, p. 1888.

Ahamed, Syeed and Glyn Davis 2009, 'Public policy and administration', in R. A. W. Rhodes (ed.), *The Australian Study of Politics*, Palgrave Macmillan, Basingstoke, UK, pp. 212–26.

Aly, Waleed 2007, *People Like Us: How arrogance is dividing Islam and the West*. Picador, Sydney.

Aroney, Nicholas, Scott Prasser and J. R. Nethercote (eds) 2008, *Restraining Elective Dictatorship: The upper house solution?* University of Western Australia Press, Crawley.

Atkinson, Alan 1993, *The Muddle-Headed Republic*, Oxford University Press, Melbourne.

Australian Human Rights Commission 2009a, *National Human Rights Consultation Report*, Australian Human Rights Commission, Canberra.

Australian Human Rights Commission 2009b, *Our Future in Our Hands: Creating a sustainable national representative body for Aboriginal and Torres Strait Islander peoples*, Australian Human Rights Commission, Sydney.

Bagehot, Walter 1872, *The English Constitution*, Second edition, Dolphin, Garden City, UK.

Barns, Greg and Anna Krawec-Wheaton 2006, *An Australian Republic*, Scribe Short Books, Melbourne.

Baylis, Thomas A. 1989, *Governing by Committee: Collegial leadership in advanced societies*, State University of New York Press, Albany.

Bean, Clive 2005, 'Is there a crisis of trust in Australia?', in Shaun Wilson, Gabrielle Meagher, Rachel Gibson, David Denemark and Mark Western (eds), *Australian Social Attitudes: The first report*, UNSW Press, Sydney.

Beer, Samuel H. 1973, 'The modernization of American federalism', *Publius*, vol. 3, no. 2 (Fall), pp. 49–95.

Bogdanor, Vernon 1995, *The Monarchy and the Constitution*, Oxford University Press, UK.

Boyce, Peter 2008, *The Queen's Other Realms: The crown and its legacy in Australia, Canada and New Zealand*, The Federation Press, Annandale, NSW.

Braithwaite, John 1997, 'On speaking softly and carrying sticks: neglected dimensions of republican separation of powers', *University of Toronto Law Journal*, vol. 47, pp. 1–57.

Braithwaite, John 1998, 'Institutionalizing distrust; enculturating trust', in Valerie Braithwaite and Margaret Levi (eds), *Trust and Governance*, Russell Sage, New York, pp. 343–75.

Braithwaite, John 2008, *Regulatory Capitalism: How it works, ideas for making it work better*, Edward Elgar, Cheltenham, UK.

Brown, A. J. 2008, 'What is a national integrity system? From temple blueprint to hip-pocket guide', in Brian W. Head, A. J. Brown and Carmel Connors (eds), *Promoting Integrity: Evaluating and improving public institutions*, Ashgate, Farnham, UK, pp. 33–52.

Brown, A.J. and Jennifer Bellamy (eds) 2007, *Federalism and Regionalism in Australia: New Approaches, New Institutions?* ANZSOG Monograph. ANU E Press, Canberra.

Cassirer, Ernst 1946 [1963], *The Myth of the State*, [Fifth edition], Yale University Press, New Haven, Conn.

Chief Justices of Australia 1997, *Statement of Independence*, Chief Justices of Australia, Perth.

Choudhry, Sujit and Bernadette Mount 2006, *Ackerman's higher lawmaking in comparative constitutional perspective: constitutional moments as constitutional failures?*, Bepress Legal Series, Paper 1544.

Cochrane, Peter 2006, *Colonial Ambition: Foundations of Australian Democracy*, Melbourne University Press, Carlton.

Coleman, Robert 1988, *Above Renown: The biography of SirHenry Winneke*, Macmillan, South Melbourne.

Constitution Commission Victoria 2002, *A House for Our Future*, Government Printer, Melbourne.

Cowan, Zelman 1985, 'The office of governor-general', in Stephen R. Graubard (ed.), *Australia: The Daedalus symposium*, Angus & Robertson, North Ryde, NSW.

Dahl, Robert 1971, *Polyarchy*, Yale University Press, New Haven, Conn.

Davis, S. Rufus 1995, *Theory and Reality: Federal ideas in Australia, England and Europe*, University of Queensland Press, St Lucia.

Eisler, Riane 1987, *The chalice and the blade: Our history, our future*, Harper and Row, San Francisco.

Eisler, Riane 1995, *Sacred Pleasure: Sex, Myth, and the Politics of the Body*, Harper, San Francisco.

Elgie, Robert (ed.) 2004, *Semi-Presidentialism in Europe*, Oxford University Press, Oxford.

Elgie, Robert and Sophia Moestrup (eds) 2007, *Semi- Presidentialism Outside Europe: A comparative study*, Routledge, London.

Elgie, Robert and Sophia Moestrup (eds) 2008, *Semi- Presidentialism in Central and Eastern Europe*, Palgrave Macmillan, Basingstoke, UK.

Fenna, Alan 2009, 'Federalism', in R. A. W. Rhodes (ed.), *The Australian Study of Politics*, Palgrave Macmillan, Basingstoke, UK, pp. 146–59.

Fitzgerald, Tony 2010, 'Power but little glory in polluted politics', *The Age Insight*, 13 March 2010, p. 9.

Friedrich, Carl 1963, *Man and His Government: An empirical theory of politics*, McGraw Hill, New York.

Fukuyama, Francis 1995, *Trust: The social virtues and the creation of prosperity*, Hamish Hamilton, London.

Galligan, Brian 1991, 'Australia', in David Butler and D. A. Low (eds), *Sovereigns and Surrogates: Constitutional heads of state in the Commonwealth*, Macmillan, London, pp. 61–107.

Galligan, Brian 1995, *A Federal Republic: Australia's constitutional system of government*, Cambridge University Press, UK.

Galligan, Brian 1999, 'The republican referendum', *Quadrant*, October, pp. 46–52.

Geertz, Clifford 1983, 'Centers, kings and charisma: reflections on the symbolics of power', *Local Knowledge: Further essays in interpretive anthropology*, Basic Books, New York, pp. 121–46.

Geertz, Clifford 2000, *Available Light: Anthropological reflections on philosophical topics*, Princeton University Press, NJ.

Green, Sir Guy 2006a, 'The marginalisation of the law in Australia: The Order of Australia Oration, 2006', *Brief* [Journal of the Law Society of Western Australia], vol. 33, no. 4 (May).

Green, Sir Guy 2006b, 'Governors, democracy and the rule of law', *Constitutional Law and Policy Review*, vol. 9, no. 1 (June), pp. 11–16, [this is a revised version of the 1999 Menzies Oration delivered by Green at the University of Melbourne].

Griffith, Gareth 2005, *Parliament and accountability: the role of parliamentary oversight bodies*, Briefing Paper no. 12/05, NSW Parliamentary Library Research Service, Sydney.

Griffith University Institute for Ethics, Governance and Law and Transparency International 2005, *Chaos or Coherence: Strengths, opportunities and challenges for Australia's integrity systems*, NISA, Brisbane.

Halligan, John and John Power 1992, *Political Management in the 1990s*, Oxford University Press, Melbourne.

Halligan, John, Robin Miller and John Power 2007, *Parliament in the Twenty-First Century: Institutional reform and emerging roles*, Melbourne University Press, Carlton.

Hamer, David 1994, *Can Responsible Government Survive in Australia?*, University of Canberra.

Hasluck, Paul, 1979 *The Office of the Governor- General*, Melbourne University Press, Carlton South.

Hayden, Bill 2008, 'Foreword' in Nicholas Aroney, Scott Prasser and J.R. Nethercote (eds), *Restraining Elective Dictatorship: The upper house solution?*, University of Western Australia Press, Crawley. pp. ix--xiii.

Head, Brian W., A. J. Brown and Carmel Connors (eds) 2008, *Promoting Integrity: Evaluating and improving public institutions*, Farnham, Ashgate, UK.

Hennessy, Peter 1995, *The Hidden Wiring: Unearthing the British Constitution*, Victor Gollancz, London.

Hirst, John 1994, *A Republican Manifesto*, Oxford University Press, Melbourne.

Holmes, Leslie 2009, 'Comparative government and politics', in R. A. W. Rhodes (ed.), *The Australian Study of Politics*, Palgrave Macmillan, Basingstoke, UK, pp. 238–56.

Irving, Helen 2009, 'The constitution and the judiciary', in R. A. W. Rhodes (ed.), *The Australian Study of Politics*, Palgrave Macmillan, Basingstoke, UK, pp. 107–18.

Keane, John 2003, *Global civil society?* Cambridge University Press, Cambridge.

Keane, John 2009, *The Life and Death of Democracy*, Simon & Schuster, London.

Kercher, Bruce 1995, *An unruly child: a history of law in Australia*, Allen and Unwin, St. Leonards.

King, Anthony 2001, *Does the United Kingdom Still Have a Constitution?*, Sweet and Maxwell, London.

Kiser, Larry L. and Elinor Ostrom 1982, 'The three worlds of action: a metatheoretical synthesis of institutional approaches', in Elinor Ostrom (ed.), *Strategies of Political Inquiry*, Sage Publications, Beverly Hills, Calif.

Kukathas, Chandran, David W. Lovell and William Maley 1990, *The Theory of Politics: An Australian perspective*, Longman Cheshire, Melbourne.

Little, Adrian 2008, *Democratic piety : complexity, conflict and violence*, Edinburgh University Press, Edinburgh.

Low, N. P. and , J. M. Power 1984, *Policy Systems in an Australian Metropolitan Region: Political and economic determinants of change in Victoria*, Pergamon Press, Oxford, UK.

Lundy, Miranda 2002, *Sacred Geometry*, Walker and Company, New York.

McGarvie, Richard E. 1999, *Democracy: Choosing Australia's republic*, Melbourne University Press, Carlton South.

Marsh, Ian and David Yencken 2004, *Into the Future: The neglect of the long term in Australian politics*, Black Inc., Melbourne.

Montesquieu, Baron de 1748 [1962], *The Spirit of the Laws*, Translated by Thomas Nugent, Hafner, New York.

Mulgan, Geoff 2006, *Good and Bad Power: The ideals and betrayals of government*, Penguin, London.

Nelson, Helen 2008, 'Public employment and multilevel governance in unitary and federal systems', in Hans-Ulrich Derlien and B. Guy Peters (eds), *The State at Work. Volume 2: Comparative public service systems*, Edward Elgar, Cheltenham, UK, pp. 33–64.

O'Brien, Patrick 1995, *The People's Case: Democratic and anti- democratic ideas in Australia's constitutional debate*, Constitutional Press, Perth.

Parliament of Australia 2004, *The Road to a Republic*, Senate Legal and Constitutional References Committee, The Senate, Canberra.

Parliament of Australia 2009a, *Plebiscite for an Australian Republic Bill 2008*, Senate Finance and Public Administration Standing Committee, The Senate, Canberra.

Parliament of Australia 2009b, *Australia's Judicial System and the Role of Judges*, Senate Legal and Constitutional References Committee, The Senate, Canberra.

Patapan, Haig 2000, *Judging Democracy: The new politics of the High Court of Australia*, Cambridge University Press, UK.

Patmore, Glenn 2009, *Choosing the Republic*, UNSW Press, Sydney.

Pettit, Philip 1997, *Republicanism: A theory of freedom and government*, Clarendon Press, Oxford, UK.

Podger, Andrew 2007, 'What really happens: department secretary appointments, contracts and performance pay in the Australian Public Service', *Australian Journal of Public Administration*, vol. 66, issue 2 (June), pp. 131–47.

Power, John 2005, An Irish style presidency for Australia?, Paper read at the Contemporary Europe Research Centre, University of Melbourne.

Power, John 2006, 'Integrity and assurance', *The Copernican Gazette*, no. 1 (Autumn), pp. 7–8.

Power, John 2008a, Managing the dual mandate problem, Paper presented to 2008 Conference of the Public Policy Network.

Power, John 2008b, A discipline colonised by a policy community? Semi-presidentialism and Australian political science, Paper presented to seminars at Victoria University of Wellington, Massey University (Albany Campus) and the University of Canberra.

Power, John 2009, 'Public administration: reflections of an old institutionalist', in R. A. W. Rhodes (ed.), *The Australian Study of Politics*, Palgrave Macmillan, Basingstoke, UK, pp. 383–9.

Power, John 2010, Monitory democracy—or a monitory branch of a democratic regime?, Paper presented to 2010 Conference of the Public Policy Network.

Power, John (Forthcoming), 'Fiducial governance: heads of state and monitory branches', submitted to *Administration and Society*.

Prasser, Scott, J. R. Nethercote and Nicholas Aroney 2008, 'Upper houses and the problem of elective dictatorship', in Nicholas Aroney, Scott Prasser and J. R. Nethercote (eds), *Restraining Elective Dictatorship: The upper house solution?*, University of Western Australia Press, Crawley, pp. 1–8.

Report of the Review of Public Service Personnel Management in Victoria 1990, Government Printer, Melbourne.

Republic Advisory Committee, *An Australian Republic*, Vols 1 and 2 1993, Commonwealth Government Printer, Canberra.

Rhodes, R. A. W. 1997, '"Shackling the leader?" Coherence, capacity and the hollow crown', in Patrick Weller, Herman Bakvis and R. A. W. Rhodes (eds), *The Hollow Crown: Countervailing trends in core executives*, Macmillan, Basingstoke, UK, pp. 198–223.

Rhodes, R. A. W. (ed.) 2009, *The Australian Study of Politics*, Palgrave Macmillan, Basingstoke, UK.

Rhodes, R. A. W. and John Wanna 2009, 'The executives', in R. A. W. Rhodes (ed.), *The Australian Study of Politics*, Palgrave Macmillan, Basingstoke, UK, pp. 119–30.

Rohr, John A. 1995, *Founding Republics in France and America: A study in constitutional governance*, University Press of Kansas, Lawrence.

Rosenau, James N. 1992, 'Governance, order and change in world politics', in James N. Rosenau and Ernst-Otto Czempiel (eds), *Governance Without Government: Order and change in world politics*, Cambridge University Press, UK, pp. 1–29.

Sawer, Marian, Norman Abjorensen and Phil Larkin 2009, *Australia: The state of democracy*, The Federation Press, Sydney.

Schumpeter, Joseph 1954, *Capitalism, Socialism and Democracy*, Allen and Unwin, London.

Sciulli, David 1992, *Theory of Societal Constitutionalism: Foundations of a non-Marxist critical theory*, Cambridge University Press, UK.

Shklar, Judith N. 1987, *Montesquieu*, Oxford University Press, UK.

Siaroff, Alan 2003, 'Comparative presidencies: the inadequacy of the presidential, semi-presidential and parliamentary distinction', *European Journal of Political Research*, vol. 42, no. 3, pp. 287–312.

Smith, Sir David 2005, *Head of State: The governor-general, the monarchy, the republic and the Dismissal*, Macleay Press, Sydney.

Spigelman, Jim 2004, The integrity branch of government, The First Lecture in the 2004 National Lecture Series for the Australian Institute of Administrative Law, Sydney.

Spigelman, Jim 2005, Judicial review and the integrity branch of government address, Paper delivered to the World Jurist Association Congress, Shanghai, September 2005.

Stewart, J. D. 1974, *The Responsive Local Authority*, C. Knight, London.

Sundquist, James L. 1992, *Constitutional Reform and Effective Government*, Revised edition, The Brookings Institution, Washington, DC.

Tan, Kevin 1997, 'The election of a president in a parliamentary system: choosing a pedigree or a hybrid?', in Kevin Tan and Lan Peng Er (eds), *Managing Political Change in Singapore: The elected presidency*, Routledge, London, ch. 4.

Thompson, Norma 2001, *The Ship of State: Statecraft and politics from Ancient Greece to democratic America*, Yale University Press, New Haven, Conn.

Tilly, Charles 2005, *Trust and Rule*, Cambridge University Press, New York.

Tsebelis, George and Money, Jeannette 1997, *Bicameralism*, Cambridge University Press, UK.

Turnbull, Malcolm 1993, *The Reluctant Republic*, Heinemann, Port Melbourne.

Turnbull, Malcolm 1999, *Fighting for the Republic: The ultimate insider's account*, Hardie Grant, South Yarra, Vic.

Uhr, John 1998, *Deliberative Democracy in Australia: The changing place of parliament*, Cambridge University Press, UK.

Uhr, John 1999, 'Introduction', in John Uhr (ed.), *The Case for Yes*, The Federation Press, Annandale, NSW, pp. 1–7.

Uhr, John 2005, *Terms of Trust: Arguments over ethics in Australian government*, UNSW Press, Sydney.

Uhr, John 2008, 'Bicameralism and democratic deliberation', in Nicholas Aroney, Scott Prasser and J. R. Nethercote (eds), *Restraining Elective Dictatorship: The upper house solution?*, University of Western Australia Press, Crawley, pp. 11–27.

Uhr, John 2009, 'Parliaments', in R. A. W. Rhodes (ed.), *The Australian Study of Politics*, Palgrave Macmillan, Basingstoke, UK, pp. 131–45.

Vile, M. J. C. 1967, *Constitutionalism and the Separation of Powers*, Clarendon Press, Oxford, UK.

Watson, Don 2002, *Recollections of a Bleeding Heart: A portrait of Paul Keating, PM*, Knopf, Milsons Point, NSW.

Whitlam, Gough 1998, 'Paul Hasluck in Australian history', in Tom Stannage, Kay Saunders and Richard Nile (eds), *Paul Hasluck in Australian History: Civic personality and public life*, University of Queensland Press, St Lucia, pp. 4–12.

Winterton, George 1994, *Monarchy to Republic: Australian republican government*, Oxford University Press, Melbourne.

Winterton, George 2004, 'The evolving role of the Governor-General', *Quadrant*, March, pp. 42–6.

Wolin, Sheldon S. 1996, 'Fugitive democracy', in Seyla Benhabib (ed.), *Democracy and Difference: Contesting the boundaries of the political*, Princeton University Press, NJ, pp. 31–45.

Zines, Leslie 2008, *The High Court and the Constitution*, Fifth edition, The Federation Press, Sydney.

Index

www.ingramcontent.com/pod-product-compliance
Lightning Source LLC
Chambersburg PA
CBHW061247270326
41930CB00033B/3487